A Taco Testimony

A Taco Testimony

Meditations on Family, Food and Culture

Denise Chávez

RIO NUEVO PUBLISHERS

TUCSON, ARIZONA

Rio Nuevo Publishers®

P.O. Box 5250, Tucson, Arizona 85703-0250

(520) 623-9558, www.rionuevo.com

Library of Congress Cataloging-in-Publication Data

Chávez, Denise.

A taco testimony : meditations on family, food and culture / by Denise Chávez.

p. cm.

ISBN-13: 978-1-887896-94-8 (pbk.)

ISBN-10: 1-887896-94-5 (pbk.)

1. Chávez, Denise—Family. 2. Mexican Americans—New Mexico—Las Cruces—Social life
and customs—20th century. 3. Mexican Americans—Food—New Mexico—Las Cruces. 4.
Mexican Americans—New Mexico—Las Cruces—Ethnic identity. 5. Las Cruces (N.M.)—
Civilization—20th century. 6. Tacos—New Mexico—Las Cruces. 7. Mexican American cook-
ery. 8. Food habits—United States. 9. Food preferences—United States. 10. Chavez family.
I. Title.

F804.L27C47 2006

394.1'209789—dc22

2006007343

Design: Karen Schober, Seattle, Washington.

Printed in Canada.

10   9   8   7   6   5   4   3   2   1

For my mother, Delfina Rede Faver Chávez
La Muchacha del Maíz Azul

"No nomás los pobres comen tacos."
"Not only the poor eat tacos."

—ROBERTO FRIETZE

Leyenda Huichol/Huichol Legend
La Madre del Maíz/The Corn Mother

… la Madre del Maíz cambió su forma de paloma y adoptó la humana; le presentó al mucha-cho sus cinco hijas, que simbolizan los cinco colores sagrados del maíz: blanco, rojo, amar-illo, moteado y azul. Como el joven tenía hambre, la Madre de Maíz le dío una olla llena de tortillas y una jícara llena de atole; él no creía que eso pudiera saciar su hambre, pero las tor-tillas y el atole se renovaban mágicamente, de manera que no podía acabárselos. La Madre del Maíz le pidió que escogiera a una de sus hijas y él tomó a la Muchacha del Maíz Azul, la más bella y sagrada de todos …

… The Mother of the Maíz changed her form from that of a dove and adopted human form; she presented to the boy her five daughters, who symbolized the five sacred colors of maíz: white, red, yellow, speckled and blue. As the young man was hungry, the Mother of the Maíz gave him a pot full of tortillas and a jar of atole; he didn't think it would sate his hunger, but the tortillas and the atole magically renewed themselves so much so that he couldn't finish them. The Mother of the Maíz requested that he pick one of her daughters. He selected the Blue Corn Girl, the most beautiful and sacred of all …

contents

MENÚ/MENU

To the Reader

This is not a sweet little book about tacos; it remembers the fights that began at the kitchen table, spilled into the dining room, then moved quickly into the living room and continued into the bedroom with the sudden slam of a door that led to the hushed sound of someone crying behind that door.

It is also about the joyful, exultant times, our nights around my Mother's round Taco Table and the generosity of spirit and love that can live in families.

It's about the living and the dead and the eternal nourishment that comes from being part of a community. Your family never leaves you and you never leave them. And in that knowing there is great blessing.

This is a memoir of food. As such, it is funny, sad, merciful and full of prayers. I hope you will enjoy some of the recipes and learn from others.

At all times you should remember where the book is set, on the U.S./México border, where one daily navigates the realities of an always changing world.

In this book I have chosen to capitalize the names of my Mother and Father. I have done this to pay honor to my parents, elevating them from their plane of existence as normal, everyday characters in a sweet little book about tacos, to the echelon of spirit ancestors where they now reside. I have done this intentionally and with full knowledge that I may have broken some grammatical rules. I have also chosen to capitalize the names of the Blue Room and the Taco Table, as well as Culture sometimes with a capital C. By doing so, I also give them honor and attention.

This isn't a formal cookbook, although there are some good recipes. If you want something more traditional, go find the cookbook section at your local independent bookstore or talk to someone in your family. And if you haven't started gathering the recipes, then someone should. My meditations are just that, ruminations on a life lived among tacos. This book has allowed me to look deeply into the history and beliefs of my family, as well as my own beliefs, and to see how alike they are and how they differ. It has provided me with a better understanding of the unique culture that is southern New Mexico, Far West Texas and northern México— alternate sides of the tortilla to you, life and sustenance to me.

Not everyone knows that there are two sides of a tortilla and that the side that hits the comal/griddle first is called "la cara/the face" and that la cara should go inside when you roll a taco, at least according to my Mother, Delfina Rede Faver Chávez.

Have you always wondered what the difference is between a taco and a flauta? New to comida Nuevo Mexicana or just haven't learned to cook tacos? Have you ever wondered why some tacos are flaky and flyaway and why the meat is all over the place? On a diet and interested in low-carb tacos? This book might answer some of those questions. I think it raises more issues than answers and that's probably good.

You might be inspired to learn to make corn tortillas "a mano," by hand, as well as begin to understand the history of maíz/corn, and by doing so, encounter and embrace a rich and wonderful culinary and cultural legacy.

Perhaps you will see your family in these stories and find mercy and forgiveness in your heart for them. For others, this book might create a space where people of all ages and backgrounds find the commonalities of universal culture as they celebrate the unique foods of any given culture, and come to a respectful and healthy understanding of who we are as global citizens.

My hope is to show how tacos have been nourishment to me, as well as a celebration of hope. I want to show how fiercely our family loved each other and how much culture has meant to me all my life. Culture with a capital C. Culture that doesn't kill, maim, degrade or believe anyone should die that we should live.

Family, food and culture are our salvation. If we have all three, we know what it is to love and value any form of life, either past, present or to come.

I honor all who sat around the round table in our dining room at home and shared with me the good, the hard, the unforgettable times.

My meditations begin in gratitude.

QUESTIONS TO PONDER:
Who ate the first taco? How was it prepared?
How much did it cost?

The Blue Room and the Nights
at the Round Table

One of my first memories is of tacos, my Mother's tacos. I am in what we called the Blue Room, what was later to become the TV room of our first and only home.

When I think of home, it is always my Mother who comes to mind. I can only think of her in capital letters. She was never mom, always Mother. To even write her name demands the respect of a capital M.

A very formal and traditional Mexican American woman who grew up in a time when the relationship between parents and children was sacrosanct, she ruled our lives by the power of her very name.

When I think of her, she stands in the unearthly, heavenly light of the Blue Room in an elegant black dress that accentuates her lush figure. She wears silver teardrop earrings, a necklace of a similar design and a bracelet—a matching set from Taxco, México. It is freshly polished with baking soda, her medicinal cure-all and her favorite housecleaning tool.

Most of Mother's jewelry was from "those days," when she was a student for thirteen summers in México City at UNAM, the National University of México. México was her heart-and-soul country, a place she loved with an abiding passion. As she swirled around the room offering this person or that one of her famous, well-loved tacos, I knew she was different from all the other mothers, all the other women of her age, of any age, from every American or Mexican or Mexican American I knew. Sadly, it wasn't until much too late that I fully came to appreciate how very special a person she was.

At that time Mother was a hardworking Spanish teacher, part-time mother, full-time wife and extraordinary hostess. She greeted all our guests effusively in either English or Spanish or both in her embracing and loving way as she danced around the room, now carrying a drink, now a heaping plate of her crisp, freshly baked, cheese-covered tacos.

In my fondest memories, the light filters through the round blue window of my favorite room of my parents' house. The bright pink walls, in combination with the cobalt light of the circular glass window, reflect a purplish-blue glow. Everyone who enters the room loves how its ethereal blue light envelops him or her with a sense of peace.

Two round windows, one blue, one white, are on opposite sides of the room. One window, the blue, faces our small street, the white one, a vacant lot. The stucco walls, with their undulating waves, not only reflect the workman's expert trowel, but remind me that this home was built by family for family. There is an otherworldly energy that emanates from the Blue Room, something profound, yet comfortable. The mysterious blue light anchors people in the everyday spiritual, the everyday real.

The blue window came from Juárez, México, forty-two miles southeast of our home in Las Cruces, New Mexico, a small city on the frontera, the border between Texas, New Mexico and northern México.

The blue window was my Mother's touch. A local workman, most likely a transplanted Mexicano, fashioned what was to become one of our house's out-standing features. Between my Mother's careful instructions and the watchful eye of my Uncle Sammie, a colonel in the National Guard, the blue glass was pared down little by little to make a nearly perfect circle. There wasn't anything mechanical or architectural my uncle couldn't do or build or patch. And except for one tiny chip on the bottom portion of the circle, hidden to all, the window was perfect.

My Father, Epifanio Ernesto, "E. E.," "Chano," Ernie, Ernest, Mr. C., or just plain Daddy, the man of many names and personalities, was a brilliant lawyer; he used his mind, his voice and his dogged intensity to influence and win people to his side. However, he had no practical living skills; he only knew how to heat canned tomato soup or fry his favorite meal, chorizo/Mexican sausage, in my Mother's favorite sartén, her beloved frying pan, and then make a plate full of tacos. Once he fed us so many chorizo tacos we all got sick.

The two brothers were very different, but the thing they had most in common was their ability to see things bigger than life with all the details. My Father, alas, was the dreamer, his brother the doer. If I saw my Mother in capital letters, the world saw my Father the same; he was the hometown boy who'd done good, the one who got away, the kid who made a name for himself; he was the successful lawyer, the son primed for greatness.

My uncle Sammie built our house with lovely hardwood floors, curved ceilings and a brick fireplace. The rooms were small, but when I was a child they seemed large, ample enough for a family of five: my Mother; my Father; my older half-sister, Faride; my younger sister, Margo; and me.

My Mother was a widow with a nine-year-old daughter when she first met my Father. I've had the grace of visiting the grave of my Mother's first husband, Tiburcio "Bucho" Faver, a descendant of the illustrious Faver family of Far West Texas, and thanking him for leaving my Mother when he did. When my sister Faride was three days old, her father died in a dark room across the courtyard of an old and rambling house in Shafter, Texas.

My Mother's wasn't an easy life, and until she met my Father, E. E. "Chano" Chávez, nine years later, she said she cried herself to sleep every night.

I am ten years old. I have already written my first story, a piece about the Willow Tree in our yard. In the story it is easy to imagine that my Mother was always my Father's alone. It wasn't until I was much older that I learned she'd had another husband, another life.

Not even my Mother knows my secret ambition is to be a writer. I have written the unthinkable words in my pink Pen Pal notebook along with other important facts that only I will read in my room later when I am alone:

INFORMATION CARD

My name is Denise Chávez.
I attend Holy Cross School.
I am in the fourth grade.

My teacher is Sister Cecilia Marie.

My Father is Ernest E. Chávez.

My Mother is Delfina R. Chávez.

I was born in Las Cruces, New Mexico, on August 15, 1948.

My height is 4 feet 2 inches.

My weight is 64 pounds.

The color of my hair is brown.

The color of my eyes is brown.

My favorite foods are Pizza and Tacos.

My favorite color is Blue.

My secret ambition is to be a writer.

All my life I have been trying to write my family's story. It hasn't been easy, not because I can't remember, but because I can't forget.

Moving from the embracing calm of the Blue Room into the bright white light of the living room, I pass a small blue, green and yellow stained-glass window in the corner near the fireplace. It adds a lovely touch to our warm little home. Once again, my Mother has seen to this detail. The windows were her idea and they made our home so special. All my life I was surrounded and influenced by her attention to color and beauty.

When you saw Mother, you knew at once you were in the presence of a unique human being. This not only had to do with her straight posture and fierce mind—she was also very beautiful. Mother was of medium height, yet to this day, everyone, including me, recalls her as being very tall. She was stately, and that alone added height.

When people meet me, they often say, "I thought you would be taller." There is something about the women in our family that gives the illusion of height. None of us is that tall, but we were taught by my Mother how to command a room. This odd blessing came from none other than La Mera Mera, the one and only, who always walked straight into the middle of a room, into any situation, and became the responsible one, the one whom people trusted and depended on.

And Mother was always exquisitely dressed, muy de moda, siempre. She wore hats and fur; her most prized possession was a stylish beaver coat. Her father, Eusebio Rede, caught the beavers near Ojinaga, México. A very famous furrier made the pelts into a stunning coat in San Antonio. No matter the season, she managed to look elegant even though we were always on a budget.

The budget was called my Father's drinking. Daddy was an alcoholic, and as a result of that, my Mother was never really financially secure.

This same generational DNA curse has followed me and set me smack dab in the middle of my parents' limitations and system of beliefs. I come from poor people who didn't acknowledge they were poor. I come from people who were always trying to get ahead and who did get ahead, leaving the shabby underpinnings of their life always in another room, tucked away in darkness, and yet, when the reckoning needed to be done, there was no getting away from the fact we were always struggling financially.

You would never have known this impeccably dressed woman suffered over her bills at night, at her small, messy desk, paying a dollar here, five dollars there to any one of her many creditors. Mother lived her life on layaway, on the delicate balance of her next, always-late paycheck from my Father, a man who wasn't reliable and drank nearly all his earnings. Mother's small salary as a Spanish teacher and later an elementary school teacher in the Las Cruces Public Schools was the ballast of our precarious life.

My Mother was a strikingly lovely woman. She had high cheekbones, a flawless complexion, haunting dark brown deep-set eyes with well-shaped brows. Her hair was dark brown and she wore it in a molote, a high, distinguished bun. She was never seen without her dark red lipstick, or her matching long, painted nails.

She had beautiful hands; various photographs attest to this. All in all, she was the vision of the perfect wife, the loving mother and impeccable hostess in her crisp apron edged in fluffy white lace, an apron she herself had made.

Mother was a wonderful seamstress, a skill she learned from her mother, Antonia Luján Rede. This is where the DNA failed me. I can't sew, never could, despite lessons from Mrs. Consuelo "Connie" Lerma, a sweet, enthusiastic sewing teacher who tried valiantly one summer to teach me how to make a dress. It was an ugly mess, starting with the material: a weak, unappealing pastel print in various shades of blue and white, with strangely shaped sailboats scattered here and there on a murky grey sea. I would have much preferred a solid color, like my friend Agnes' sleeveless burgundy linen dress that fit her athletic figure so well. Next to her, my sailboats floundered in a sea of angst.

I was a tormented girl. Nothing ever quite fit, was ever enough. Everything connected to family was too familiar and as a result, too strange. All I wanted in those days was solitude and peace, to be left alone, to move far away from family, most of whom I found to be a curious lot.

Mother was a schoolteacher and this made our life very visible to many people. Everyone knew my Father, the lawyer, as well. He was the assistant District Attorney and highly respected. Mother's record was irreproachable, and she was highly regarded by all her students and colleagues. And of course, everyone knew my grandfather and grandmother, my uncles, my aunts, and at least one generation of cousins, mostly female. When speaking of family, we spoke of generations first. Everyone knew what street I lived on and how I was either related to him or her or how I wasn't. And if I wasn't, why not?

My parents were still together then, we were a family for a while, and our magic consisted in the glow that emanated from the blue window in the Blue Room that created our dreamland, our fantasy landscape, the other, better world where each of us went to become whole, as we glossed over and then dismissed the broken selves we, in fact, really were.

Another of my sacred memories is sitting in our dining room during one of our many nights at the round table, the Taco Table, as my Mother served food to our guests. This memory is as important to me as when my Father took my sister Margo and me to eat our first pizza in Albuquerque. I remember how excited I was, how happy we both were to be with our Father, going out to eat something exotic, new. We had no pizzerias in Las Cruces and depended on Chef Boyardee instant homemade pizzas. Neither did we have Chinese food. Mother occasionally treated us to cans of Chun King chicken and vegetables with crispy chow mein noodles. There was something celebratory about this special food in my life. And tacos never took a back seat to any of the other food. Tacos for me have never, ever been ordinary. Just as that first pizza, Chun King canned Chinese food or Chef Boyardee has never been ordinary.

———•◦•◦•———

Everything in my life then was family. Not much else mattered. And so to understand what tacos mean to me, you need to understand what family is and was.

———•◦•◦•———

Everyone who knew Mother loved her.

That is, everyone loved her except her ex-best friend, the woman who accused her of stealing my Father away from her—the jilted girlfriend who never forgave her. Despite the fact my Father was an alcoholic womanizer who was not to be trusted, the maligned woman held her stubborn grudge against my Mother all her life. When I asked my Father about his ex-girlfriend, he snorted that she was never his girlfriend, and not only that, she was delusional and a drunk.

My Father, who was known by most people including his family by his nickname "Chano," was a catch in the late 1940s. He was a handsome and talented young attorney just recently returned from Georgetown Law School in Washington, D.C. The world awaited him, his life was all promise. As the family heir designate (his older talented brother, Alejandro, having been killed on a flying mission during World War II), Chano was the one everyone knew would succeed. It was unthinkable for a young Mexican American man born on the U.S./México border in the 1920s, a young man who was punished for speaking Spanish on the school grounds with his friends, to go to school so far away and to come back with a law degree. But he didn't accomplish this feat alone. He was indebted to his mentor, New Mexico Senator Dennis Chávez, who encouraged him. It is Senator Chávez who became my padrino, who baptized me, and whose name I carry.

And yet, I often wondered why my Father returned home to New Mexico, to the poverty-stricken town he grew up in. Why did he return to his old, haunted neighborhood, Chiva Town, named for its random goats, the muss and disorder of poverty and the heat of a relentless desert? How did my Father find his way back? He once told me he was embarrassed to write the name of his street on his letters: Mesquite. "Who comes from streets with those kind of names?" he said with shame. Espina—thorn, Campo—field, Tornillo—screw. Esperanza—hope.

"Only poor wetbacks come from streets with those names," he said with disgust.

If my Father hated it so much, why did he come back to the poverty, to the dust?

The real story is that he'd been gone ten years already and somewhere back there he'd left a wife behind who really left him because he was an alcoholic. June was her name. I have possession of the divorce papers. My Father never spoke of June to me, ever, but I do have a picture of her. She was a long-legged, lovely blonde and she did once love him. And he loved her as well or he never would have married her in that place so far away from the heat and the dust, from the random goats and chickens, the squalor of Chiva Town and the memories of his sad youth. My Father still had hope then. But June was now part of his murky past, a reminder of his continuing failure to love.

Daddy had brilliant trial skills; he was a great orator, a passionate trial attorney.

"No one knew law like him," someone once said to me. "He could have been governor. Senator. He was that brilliant. If only … if only …"

The if only was, of course, my Father's curse. He was an alcoholic and there was no getting around it.

Mother used to say: "Just listen to him. He repeats the same thing over and over. There he goes again with his litany. I have so many friends … I know so and so … so and so and so and so and so and so … they're good friends of mine." I can hear my Mother ridiculing him with her worn-down, beaten and sarcastic voice, "If you have so many friends, Mr. C., what has happened to them? Where are they now?"

———◦•◦•◦———

We lived a family lie. Successful small-town lawyer, untroubled beautiful mother from an even smaller town once called El Polvo, The Dust. My Mother came out of that no man's land of Far West Texas. And my Father never let her forget it.

My Father was born in Doña Ana, New Mexico, and grew up on the poor side, the east side, the Mexican side of Las Cruces, New Mexico.

My Mother came from the thick dust of what was later to be known as Redford, Texas. Population maybe fifty.

My Father came from a family of dreamers and schemers, and for a while my Mother was part of that elusive effervescent hazy dream of his.

Back then, the glow was there. Family and friendships surrounded us all. There were so many parties at our house. We ate tacos at the round table, in the Blue Room, in the crowded kitchen, in every single room of that small house. We danced in the hallways and wept in the elegant blue tiled bathroom, alone and with each other. We rolled with laughter on the floors and slept on the sundeck until we couldn't bear the heat and came inside to shade. We lived in every single room and inhabited every corner of that yard, back and front. I knew every bush, every weed, every corner and niche of my long-standing longing in that house of longing. I wanted to go away, far away, and never come back, ever. And I wanted my Mother to be happy; above all, I wanted her to know peace and love.

I spent many nights lying on the roof looking at the solemn stars in my tucked-away perch just to the side of our huge mulberry tree and wondered who I was, where I was headed and when I could get to where I needed to go. That place. Faraway. Wherever it was.

And throughout all that time, though I didn't know it, I was happy. And safe. And loved. And there was as much peace as you can have in a house full of women without a man, a wife without a husband, daughters without a father, growing young women of increasing sexuality with an overbearing, nervous, very traditional religious Mother, two sisters mostly at odds of nearly the same age wearing almost the same dress size, another sister long gone, a family torn asunder, brought together again, always re-inventing themselves because we had to. There were celebrations of all kinds, weddings, funerals, anniversaries, birthdays. There was Valentine's Day, Easter, Halloween, Thanksgiving and Christmas. There were celebrations with and without name. And there were just ordinary days. And the food we always served was tacos, my Mother's special rolled tacos covered in cheese, just out from the oven piping hot. Watch it! An oven mitt in one hand holding a very hot tray of tacos, the other hand holding a metal spatula, the only real question was: "How many?"

PRAYER BEFORE EATING TACOS

We offer up this meal with gratitude.
We remember that tacos are one of life's greatest blessings.
We remember that tacos are sacred.

We bless the land that gives us chile, rice and beans.
We bless the vegetables that give of themselves to feed us as well: the tomatoes,
    the lettuce, the cilantro, the chiles and the onions.
We remember that family is more than family.
We remember that food is more than food.

We remember that culture is more than culture.
Family is life.
Food is life.
Culture is life.

We remember that love is the essence of all family, of all food, of all culture.
Everything to do with cooking our food is an art.
Whether it is buying the chile for the season, roasting it, putting it in bags and
    freezing it,
Whether it is taking off the skins or de-veining it,
We always remember the gift of its potency and its nourishment.

Our chile is our health.
Our tacos are our health.
Our enchiladas and our flautas are our health.

We will cook with attention.
No steps eliminated, no steps forgotten.

All is well with our bodies.
All is well with our food.

Our bodies accept our food with gratitude.
Tacos are more than tacos.
Food is more than food.
Culture is more than culture.

We are more than what we seem to be.

We are greater than what we can ever imagine.

And in that knowledge, we find peace.

Amen.

Tacos a la Delfina

I learned to make tacos from my Mother. Her tacos were unparalleled. And for this great gift I am thankful.

2 pounds hamburger meat (lean but not too lean)

1 small onion, diced

Fresh garlic

1 can (15 ounces) sweet green peas or potatoes or corn. Get a good brand. You can also use fresh peas or potatoes or corn, but you will need to boil the potatoes or corn ahead of time and dice the potatoes small.

Comino/ground cumin to taste (use sparingly as it goes a long way)

Salt to taste

Garlic powder or fresh garlic to taste

Oil for cooking tortillas

A family pack of 3 dozen corn tortillas. You never know exactly how many you are going to use. Sometimes they come folded and can't be used for the tacos, or

*you might be tempted to just heat one up and eat it
with butter. Also, you can never account for how
much meat filling you or any other taco partner will
use to fill each tortilla. Best to be on the safe side.*

*Shredded cheese, such as Longhorn, Monterey Jack,
Colby or mild Cheddar*

Fry the hamburger with the onion and fresh garlic. Don't use too lean of a meat, as you want some fat. It's worthwhile to get good meat. The better the meat, the better the taco. Avoid meat that looks as if it will never blend; sometimes when the meat is extruded by the butcher it stays in that extruded state.

Drain the peas, potatoes or corn and save the juice. You will use the juice later. Add drained peas, potatoes or corn to the meat and mash. You will need a good machacador/masher. This is the step where fledgling taco-istas go wrong. You need a "binder" for the meat. The peas, potatoes or corn serve this purpose. They will keep the meat from becoming "flyaway" or dry. How my Mother decided on peas, I will never know, but it works. The sweetness of the peas adds a great flavor and texture.

When you have mashed the meat and peas, potatoes or corn into a mash, add comino and salt. Add the additional garlic or garlic powder. Add the saved vegetable juice. You will let this mixture simmer awhile and then remove from the heat.

Cool the meat mixture as you fry the tortillas in just enough oil to soften them. Use canola oil for frying tortillas, although you may use manteca vieja, old lard or leftover cooking oil, as suggested by my friend Sylvia Bejarano, who swears by her tasty manteca. Stack the lightly fried, now soft tortillas on a plate to cool. Some people steam their tortillas or put them in the oven to heat. There are all sorts of permutations, but I prefer a soft corn tortilla that has been fried. You can pat the tortilla down to remove excess grease.

Roll tacos, cara/face to the inside, into cylinders. Remember that the cara refers to the side of the tortilla that hits the sartén first when it is cooked. It is always darker than the other side. Don't use too much or too little meat; about 2 tablespoons per taco is good. The meat should extend to almost the edge of the tortilla. Place the rolled tortillas onto a cookie sheet or flat pan and bake at 350 degrees F until they are crisp. Or you can cook them on the stove in a heavy frying pan, the manteca vieja approach. They are really tasty cooked in an old sartén, as the edges fry while the middle stays soft. If you cook the tacos in the oven they will have a general crispy-ness all over. For large groups it's best to cook tacos in the oven. Only when they are crisp should you add the cheese. Sprinkle the cheese on top, staying away from the edges. Some people like more cheese than others, so you should be generous but not overbearing. Cheese does not make a taco, but it is a good complement.

What cheese to use? A Longhorn is good, also a Monterey Jack, or a Colby mix. Mild Cheddar is good. You can blend several types.

I've known few people who haven't grabbed a quick bite of taco meat or rolled a fast taco, nomás para probar, just to "see how things are going." The fresh meat and the soft tortilla are always winners. You can mix and match a cheese taco with a meat taco. The cheese tacos made with this grated cheese are very tasty.

Serve piping hot. The next day you can heat up leftovers in a frying pan or just eat them from the refrigerator. I swear these tacos are really good cold.

Piñata Parties with Peanut Butter and Banana Sandwiches

Have you ever tasted a peanut butter and banana sandwich? If you have, you know how wonderful they can be. Just as Mother was known for her tacos, she was also famous for her peanut butter and banana sandwiches. All the kids in the neighborhood loved them. And I loved them more than anyone else.

The combination of creamy peanut butter with the sweetness of bananas is a wondrous thing. Mother would take white bread and spread peanut butter on it.

Then she would take thin banana slices and spread them over the bread. She then would cut the "bones" off the bread and save them for capirotada, her trademark bread pudding. The "bones" consisted of the darker edges of the bread, looked upon by many as too hard or too pedestrian to eat. Mother never wasted anything so precious as bread bones, and she used them either in her capirotada or as dry bread crumbs in her meat loaf.

It felt quite sophisticated for us neighborhood kids to eat sandwiches without the bones. A ragtag group of kids it was, too: my younger sister, Margo; my older sister, Faride; all the nearby cousins, males and females, including WarrenRebecca-FredLisaCharlotteLilliaBinoHeleneChilton, all from the western end of our small street that faced the Organ Mountains; my Aunt Elsie's brood; and the other cousins on the next street over, the Three Ks: Kathy, Karen and Kim Chávez, my Uncle Sammie's gang. The neighborhood kids included Irene Vlahakis, who was my older sister's age and lived with her father, Gus, at the end of the street. Her mother had died long before. And then there were the Valdéz boys and across from them the Paredes and any number of other kids that came and went and our spoiled brat neighbor, Sugar, whom my sister and I adored, and the Mendoza kids, including the neighborhood nemesis, "Bad Elmo," who punched in our plastic swimming pool and tormented us with his boyish pranks.

All of these kids, or permutations of them, gathered at our house for birthday parties that included three standard items: tacos for the adults, peanut butter and banana sandwiches for the kids and a piñata for everyone. We'd congregate in the back yard, where my Father had rigged up a long rope that hung from the top of the roof and came down over the back wall of the house and held a colorful piñata in place—a graceful swan or the traditional Mexican multi-colored star. All the kids yelped and pranced as my Father held sway over that rope—bouncing the piñata up and down as it flittered in the hot summer air as we children tried to hit it, blindfolded, full of ourselves.

Peanut Butter and Banana Sandwiches

1 or more loaves of soft, white bread. Forget whole wheat, kids don't like it.

Creamy peanut butter

Bananas as needed

Toothpicks

Take a loaf of soft, white bread and cut off the bones.

Save the bones in a plastic bag for capirotada or meat loaf.

Spread creamy peanut butter on two slices of bread.

Cut bananas into small rounds, not too thick.

Arrange banana rounds on bread slices.

Match slices of bread together but don't squish too much.

Cut bread into four triangles.

Put a colorful toothpick into each triangle.

Warn kids about the toothpicks.

Pass out sandwiches.

Warn kids and whatever adults are nearby about the toothpicks again.

Pick up toothpicks and monitor miniature "sword fights" between the boys.

Hand out washrags to everyone.

Pick up washrags.

Get ready for the piñata!!!

Mother bought the piñatas in Juárez at the main market, Mercado Juárez, and the candy as well—the blue, pink and white hard candy balls with bumpy surfaces, the wooden boxes of tasty cajeta, the yellow and green lollipops made of piña and chile, and various other kinds of too-sweet candy that I still love and that come from México. American candy has never been as tasty to me as Mexican candy.

Early on, I was a sugar addict and, desgraciadamente, continue to be one to this day. I'm not proud of all the candy I've snuck under my bed or into a drawer and eaten at all hours of the day and night. My Mother was the same. If you looked in one of her kitchen cabinets you were likely to find orange slices or Baby Ruths or candy corn. An early sugar memory is going into the kitchen to get my Mother's sugar cubes to suck on. Sugar has been a problem for me all my life.

I come from sugar addicts and alcoholics. And the other, younger generation has been addicted to drugs and many of them to alcohol as well. One of my cousins returned from Vietnam a heroin addict and eventually OD'd. He was a talented artist and so much more than his addiction. Like many of our family members, he sat around our kitchen and dining room table and enjoyed my Mother's tacos.

It's not surprising I like sugar, given my legacy of imbalance. My Mother's addiction was my Father. And my Father's addiction was to the drink and the dark sadness inside of him. Where did that sadness come from?

My Aunt Elsie used to say it was because he'd nearly drowned in high school when he went skinny dipping with some friends in the river, near Mesilla Dam. Several of them drowned, including his girlfriend. He almost drowned as well. She remembered him locked in his room for months, crying. "This was before therapy, Denise," she said sadly. "Why didn't we realize he needed help? Your Daddy was never the same after that. But we didn't know. It was so long ago. This was before therapy."

―――⚫―――

What does all this have to do with tacos?

This is my story of nourishment, of culture, and how I came to know who I am in the warm effervescent blueness of my Mother's desire and the cold analytical whiteness of my Father's drive, and how his handicap, his dis-ease, his inability to stay on the path, his overwhelming need to drink, drink, to forget, forget, combined with my Mother's relentless fury to remember, remember and how that combination of spirits made me who I am. My parents gifted me with that DNA, and the story of tacos is my owning of our story.

———

I stand in the sobering, almost wistful half-light of memory as my Mother distributes another taco to our party guests. She is the perfect hostess. She knows what matters, how to fulfill. I hear Daddy in the background. It is a toast to one of his friends. So and so and so and so or something or other. Glass raised high, he looks at my Mother with desire. She is beautiful and he knows it ... if only she understood him, left him alone ...

She looks back at him, her dark eyes flashing; he is the man she didn't know she was waiting for. She was a widow dressed in black for nine years, a widow with a small child, too many broken dreams. And when she finally found the one man she knew she could love, the returned hero, the family hope, her savior and love, he was a man ever unable to swim out into clear water.

"His teeth were like pearls," she said to me more than once. "They were so perfect, so white. What happened to him? Now his teeth are small, bitten down. I didn't know about him until our wedding night. No one told me. It wasn't until that evening that I realized he was an alcoholic. No one told me. He was so talented, such a good lawyer—I never knew—If only I knew. If only—"

———

For all of us Chávez there were days without tacos. Days with tacos. Tacos were then, and still are, special food. Everything that constituted a celebratory Chávez meal was memorable and not to be talked about lightly. Every element combined to make a perfect whole. The Chávez family whole. The dream family whole. The outward happy whole. The chosen whole. My Mother's all-embracing whole. The wholeness of who I still am and was, back then.

Every element of our special family dinner is to be celebrated for its unique part in making what, in my mind, is the perfect meal. In the pink-blue flush of a respite from all that lies beneath the surface, my parents were happy, ever the gracious hosts. And a party at the Chávez house in this small town was legendary, at least in my mind. No paper plates, no plastic dinnerware. Mother had been polishing her silver for days; she'd taken out all the elegant serving spoons from her two wooden silverware boxes; all the large plates and all her crystal bowls were filled with food. For us, Los Chávez de Las Cruces, another party was ready to begin.

A SPECIAL CHÁVEZ FAMILY DINNER

Tacos a la Delfina

Spanish—really Mexican—rice

Calabacita, zucchini squash with fresh corn

Frijoles a la olla

Green chile salsa

Tortillas de harina, hechos a mano, made by hand

Salad with iceberg lettuce and tomatoes, from the Mesilla Valley

Chile con queso made with Velveeta cheese

Homemade tostada chips

Iced tea, water, juice

Nothing alcoholic

Green, white and pink party mints

Mixed nuts with mostly peanuts

Marshmallow Surprise

Capirotada

Tacos with the Three Magi

Christmas was my Mother's favorite and least favorite time of the year. Mother loved to entertain, and Christmas was her time; she loved the music, the ritual and drama of Christmas. She loved decorating the house and tree and would bring out all her special ornaments that she kept in the attic and one by one would unwrap them carefully and set them out in their special places. The house was never lovelier and more decorated than at that time of year.

As a devout Catholic, she loved everything that led to Christmas, including Midnight Mass. We attended La Misa del Gallo every year, and yes, sometimes it was difficult to stay awake. If we got to Saint Genevieve's Church late, we'd likely have to stand at the back. If my Father were around, he would usually go to Mass with us. Once he stood in the back and Mother said she could identify his cough among the many. I have no doubt she could, they were so attuned to each other—or rather, she was aware of everything he did and was. She was a second skin that for him was always raw, blistering. For her, he was the slippery essence that never left her.

Mother's birthday was on December 24 and she felt she got cheated out of gifts. I don't remember that we ever had a birthday party for her. Her school chores came fast on the heels of all she did. During her brief Christmas break there was a lot to do, both inside and outside the house.

When we were young, my uncle Eddie "Lalo" Chávez, a talented but frustrated artist who worked designing commercial signs, painted three large flat panels that portrayed the journey of the Magi toward Bethlehem. They were placed on top of the roof in front of a band of homemade lights my Father rigged up out of old metal coffee cans. My older sister, Faride, would climb up on the roof and spread out the junky set of makeshift lights that my Father had made. She tells me she got an electrical shock each time she lit them. These homemade lights surrounded the Bethlehem scene and from afar, they were magical. When driving by, no one noted that the three backdrops were propped up precariously on our sloping roof and that they were prone to fall over when any strong wind came along.

The painted panels were very unusual for their time and were most likely the only such painted scenes to be found in our small town. The one on the far left depicted one of the Kings on a reclining camel laden with gifts for the Baby Jesus. The one in the middle showed the other two Kings on the backs of camels. The far right panel showed the town of Bethlehem in the distance with a bright star hovering above. The Three Kings are still a ways off from their destination, and yet, there is a sense of hope and expectancy in their poses. Why my Uncle Lalo decided to paint this scene and not the manger scene is curious. But there is a sense of mystery about the Magi as they make their way toward the Christ. All they could see in the distance was the star that beckoned them.

Our house was the first one built on the block, and for a while, we were the only house on the street. My Aunt Elsie owned the property on the street and little by little she began to sell off the lots. The surrounding fields were planted with cotton and sugar beets. Even now, as a result of this, my husband's garden is always compromised. The earth remembers cotton.

Even after other houses were built, ours was still the loveliest for a long time. Only when the Mendoza home was built, that two-story wonder situated at the end of the block near the Dairy Queen, was our house supplanted.

Our front door was decorated with blue Christmas lights, as were the rosebushes. The winding walkway leading to the house was bordered by luminarias, folded paper bags that held small votive lights. We were taught to carefully fold down the edges of each bag, placing a small amount of sand in the bottom. The small votive candle was set firmly in the middle. My younger sister and I were the designated luminaria lighters. Later, when the Three Magi and the shining star of Bethlehem were gone, there were always at least the luminarias to glow brightly through the early morning hours as the Christ Child was being born.

Inside, the house was filled with decorations. A green and red felt wreath spanned the dining room/living room archway. There were recycled Christmas glass bulbs without their proper circular metal rings that stood in bowls everywhere, defective side down. The buffet was decorated with angel hair, that silky material made of spun glass, and it was spread underneath a Nativity set that stood below a large framed print of Christ painted by someone named Sallman. Later I learned the danger of that spun glass, but in those days the house was full of angel hair in all colors: blue, white, pink. A large ceiling-high tree stood in the corner of the living room near the south-facing windows. Despite the fact that my Mother was very traditional in many ways, her Christmas trees always made a bold statement. They were either pink or silver or blue or flocked with heavy fake white snow, and among family and friends they were legendary for their whimsical creativity.

The melodic sounds of Perry Como and Bing Crosby floated from my Mother's bedroom, as well as other music: a version of "Christmas Bells" and "The Little Drummer Boy" by a little-known Christian group—records bought on sale that weren't particularly noteworthy. The Christmas music started up around Thanksgiving and went on into mid-January.

And in the middle of all this celebration were my Mother's tacos and sopaipillas.

I wish I could share a recipe for her outstanding sopaipillas. It's not possible. She used her flour tortilla masa/dough, cut it in triangles and jabbed a fork into it before she put the masa into a very hot oil-filled sartén. Mother always said you had to get the oil really hot. Her sopaipillas were fluffy and light, not at all greasy. They were memorable, as was her pan, a flatbread she made from her tortilla dough. Again, I have no recipe for this bread. It was always tasty, whether hot or cold. Pan tasted especially delicious when it was hot and you spread butter inside.

Heaven is memory, I think. To go back in time and spend one day with my Mother would be El Colmo, the be-all and end-all of happiness and blessing. I might go back on Christmas Eve, when all was preparation and fulfillment, as we trudged to La Misa del Gallo, Midnight Mass, returning home expectant but sleepy. We opened our gifts immediately after we got home. Mother loved to give us gifts, and everyone's pile was huge, except hers. After we opened our enormous pile of gifts, mostly clothing, we spread them on the blue crushed velvet living room couch, where they stayed for several days or maybe even a week. Other gifts filled the floor space underneath the tree and lay on nearby tables. After opening our gifts, we modeled everything for Mother, who gave us her critical assessment, and only then did we trudge off to bed. I would wend my way to my purple bedroom at the back of the house, where I would lie in bed feeling the deep and contented peace of someone who had it all figured out. I would finally fall asleep, knowing the deep cold was "out there" and that it would not touch me, not this night, because I was inside my warm and secure bed in my Mother's house, my Mother's blessed and sacred house.

Oh yes, I would go back to a taco-filled Christmas Eve followed by La Misa de Gallo followed by the delicious sleep that led into Christmas Day.

The next morning Mother let us sleep late, our Mass obligation fulfilled. We arose and chose one new outfit to wear for our visit to our Aunt Elsie's house, to take them gifts and visit with Granma Lupe, my Father's elderly, bedridden mother. I always marveled at my aunt and uncle's ugly, always-skinny, runty trees, their lack of ornaments. Everyone in their large family drew someone's name to give a present to. They never had piles of gifts like we did. They never had each sock, each shoe lovingly and separately wrapped the way my Mother wrapped our gifts. They never had outrageously painted trees and they never had tacos for Christmas like we did.

My Mother was generous to my Father's family and always gave them something handmade: aprons, handbags, tablecloths, scarves, a bedspread or maybe one of her handmade pillows, which were very special, until one day some rude and thoughtless person ('fess up!) said out loud for her to hear, "Here comes Delfina with her pillows."

Mother made designer suits and dresses for my sister and me. What you got as a gift depended on your status in her life. She also made quilts, but these were reserved for the very few. I still have some of her quilts, many of them shiny with use. They've kept me warm all these years, through years of many tacos and few tacos.

Entremeses/Hors d'Oeuvres

The Never-Ending Gift of Tacos

My Mother's tacos were good cold. We took them on trips short and long. One Halloween Mother didn't have money to buy candy, so we locked up the house and set off to see movies at the nearby Fiesta Drive-In. They charged $1.00 a car and for that, we were able to see a double feature. Mother figured by the time the movies were over, the trick-or-treaters would be gone. In those days there were a lot of kids who lived in the neighborhood, so an investment in candy was substantial. She decided that instead of spending money on others, we would go to the movies, and take some tacos with us. When we left the drive-in, sleepy-headed and satiated, the neighborhood was full of darkened houses and for that my Mother was relieved.

My Mother, besides loving tacos, loved hamburgers, which when you think about it are another kind of taco. She was a meat eater, and nothing made her happier than a taco or a piece of meat, well done, nearly charred.

Early on, I moved away from my Mother's hard-core meat diet. For years I have been a vegetarian, save for tacos. I would eat my meat loaf or my pot roast, or a chicken fried steak in high school or college, but for the most part, I have never really cared for beef.

As a college student at New Mexico State University, I ate a hamburger nearly every day for four years. My Mother would give us a food allowance of a dollar a day, and that would pay for a hamburger, French fries and a Dr. Pepper. Sometimes I varied my meal by ordering a grilled cheese sandwich.

In my college days, when Margo and I were in school, it was a mixture of drama people and international students who came around to eat tacos with us, as well as Father Blaise Schauer, pastor of Saint Albert the Great Newman Center, the campus ministry. Father Schauer would call up my Mother to tell her he was coming over on Thursday night or Sunday night and that he wanted tacos. He often invited guests along and often didn't tell my Mother. He loved her tacos, and so she always had a large quantity prepared because she never knew who was coming over. Also, Father Schauer had an enormous appetite. Mother always sent him home with plates of food.

We often had a priest or two join us for dinner, including Father Schauer or my Mother's friend, Father Bede O'Leary, a short, ornery monk who told latecomers in Mass that they should just leave because they were so tardy. He was intolerant and brittle, sharp-tongued and irascible. But Mother and her tacos had tamed him. Father O'Leary taught a class on the New Testament for the seventh graders at Holy Cross School, and he was my teacher. I remember receiving an A. Perhaps my

Mother's tacos had swayed him. Father O'Leary was a small, grey-looking man with a large hook nose. He and Mother often discussed the arts and theology. They seemed mismatched friends but they were quite fond of each other. The last time we saw him was at his priory in Gethsemane, Kentucky, when Mother, Margo and I paid him a visit. My sister was a widow, her young husband having died in a car accident in Germany. We drove down from her school in Brattleboro, Vermont, arriving around lunchtime, and although Father O'Leary didn't appear for a while, a young monk brought each of us a tray with a plate of food. I don't remember what the food was, but it was warm, tasty. We said grace together and I remembered all the meals we'd had with Father O'Leary at my Mother's Taco Table. This memorable meal, served out of love and in such a faraway place, was a just payment for those countless visits of that cantankerous and critical monk, my Mother's tacos his true salvation.

While I was a drama major, my sister majored in English literature. She hung out with international students and danced every year in their Mini-World Program. I was emcee for several years and knew all her friends, and sometimes our friends and worlds blended, as I attended foreign student parties and Margo took part in our theatre productions. She has always been a talented actress and writer. Both of us were always very active in our respective realms.

I remember one particular international student party when we danced to very loud cumbias in the hallway on top of the floor furnace grates between my bedroom in the back and my Mother's in front. A neighbor called the police because of the noise and my Mother, normally staid and quite circumspect, told him to go to hell. But not in public. She took him to the farthest recess of our house, which would have been my Father's old study, and chewed him out. He left, abashed and reprimanded. The dancing continued until the wee hours of the morning.

In those days the pranks were silly and without malice. Mother would often wake up to find the rosebushes in front of the house full of toilet paper. Once even her statue of St. Francis was covered with toilet paper and—God help us—someone had put an orange life vest on him. She liked the look of it, and so it stayed there a while.

My Mother really liked our friends and enjoyed serving them tacos. Those were the days when the tacos kept coming. Our friend Barthy Byrd has never forgotten how I once yelled to Mother in the kitchen to bring in more tacos. "Delfina, ¡más tacos!" Barthy loved the memory of me shouting to my Mother.

Delfina, ¡Más Tacos!

"My daughter, Denise, is yelling to me from the dining room, 'Delfina, ¡más tacos!' I call her Neesh. Neesh is calling to me. I'm in the kitchen at 480, our home. I'm frying up another batch of tacos. People have been coming over all night. It's Christmas Eve and the living room is full of people. Most of them are Margo's friends, international students from the university: from Japan, Noriko and Yoshiko; Margo's boyfriend, Michel Charles; the two Pierres (Little Pierre and Big Pierre); and Big Pierre's girl-friend, Sandy. My sobrino Antonio Luján, el travieso Brown Beret, he's out there, and in the dining room are Denise's drama friends, Charles Lewis and Irene Oliver, Barthy Byrd and Dan Case, and of course Denise, who keeps yelling to me, 'Delfina, ¡más tacos!' I can hear her yelling to me as if I were a short-order cook. And I guess I am the cook. Denise comes in with a tray, takes the tacos out. 'Delfina, ¡más tacos!'

"I'm happiest when I'm at home serving my family tacos. And it doesn't matter who is here—sometimes Father Schauer with some students from the Newman Center. He'll call me and tell me he's coming over such and such a night and can I make some tacos? That is what he wants, what he always asks for. Tacos! Tacos!

"Do I ever get tired of tacos? No! I love tacos! I love to fix tacos for my family, for their friends, for Father Schauer or Father O'Leary. He eats so little and is so picky, not like Father Schauer. And course, everyone loves my sopaipillas. They're famous! No one else's sopaipillas are as light and fluffy as mine. Well, most of the time. Sometimes they are flat and leaden, but it's rare. The secret has to do with the baking powder, la espauda.

"'Delfina, ¡más tacos!' Denise calls to me. My girls are home. Safe. Happy.

"If only Ernest were here. Where is Mr. C. now? Ay, que Dios lo cuide. Where could he be?

"'Delfina, ¡más tacos!'

"¡Ahí voy, ahí voy! I'm coming, I'm coming!"

Tacos, Tacos, Tacos

When I think of tacos, I see my Mother cooking in her blue and pink tiled kitchen. I used to perch on the blue linoleum counter by the stove and watch her cook. A nearby radio was tuned to XELO, the Mexican station. Emilia, my Mother's ayudante/helper, a short, white-haired older woman from Juárez who lived with us for some time, stirred a pot of beans and helped my Mother cook. Like my Mother, she also made wonderful tortillas. And she was kind. For some reason, we once got on a Tilt-a-Whirl ride at the carnival together. I can't imagine why this would happen, but it did. I didn't imagine this scenario, although it seems dream-like. The bar holding us to our seats came loose. Emilia grabbed me and pulled me back onto the seat. She was steady, immovable, solid as a mountain. I never mentioned this to anyone, nor did she speak to me about the potential accident. I think I could have been badly injured, but instead she saved me. I just can't understand why we were on that ride together. It seems so incongruous. I hated carnival rides; they scared me.

Once my younger sister and I were so scared we started praying the rosary on something called the Octopus. We got on the rides because my Father used to take us to the carnival, and he imagined we liked the rides. Once he left us on a Ferris wheel for a number of revolutions beyond the one we thought he had paid for. He didn't tell us about it nor did he apologize afterward when we got off, two small frightened girls, crying their eyes out. We thought he had forgotten us, and he just wanted to give us a good, long ride. My Father was thoughtless in that way. In his desire to please and make up for things, he often hurt people.

Emilia was the representation of that time, the culture, the food. She was our friend, our sister, our ayudante, and she took care of us when my Mother taught school. I have remembered her in my poem Tilt-A-Whirl.

TILT-A-WHIRL

Sliding down
Emilia
I was falling from that thrill machine
nearby sister pressed between two fat cousins

Your great tortilla hands
sustained me
you folded me up
set me back down
on the metal seat
a trembling child
and who would ever know
that fear
but me and you:
Mexican Indian without words
and a lifetime of work
behind you

Greyed jackal
at the gate of death
without thinking

you turned me back
to colored lights
the carnival
as easily as flipping
a tortilla from the heat

Vengan a comer las tortillas
ya están listas
turn and turn and turn
she said
this is the secret
instead of islands you have worlds

Few people will tell you that the secret of tortillas is in the turn of the tortilla. I should know, because mine always looked like Cuba. I could never make a perfectly round tortilla; they always looked like misshapen islands. Emilia had the turn right and so did my Mother. I, alas, never learned the magic turn!

———•·•·•———

The art of cooking comida Mexicana is something many imagine they have mastered, but they haven't. If you go on the Internet you can see thousands of entries for tacos. Some websites have pictures and others offer recipes. There are recipes for Choco Tacos/chocolate tacos, any number of dessert tacos, recipes for tacos al pastor, for salsas and "ta-kee-toes," or "ray-on-ohs" … You name it, someone has a good or a better recipe for any type of Mexican food.

For some people, flautas are double tacos and burritos are soft tacos.

Others will extol the use of lime. I, too, would add my respectful salute to the magnificent limón/lime. Lime is very important in all Mexican cooking. It revs things up, wakes up the food! Sometimes you can feel a taco overload if you don't remember the basics. Tacos are tacos when they're tacos. But not all tacos are alike. What keeps me steady and grounded is that I know tacos. Real tacos. Tacos de deveras.

Tacos de Sobritas/Leftover Tacos

Anyone knows that tacos can heal any cruda, any horrendous hangover. I should know.

In my college days, I drank a lot. A group of us would drive to Juárez, without permission and against my Mother's wishes, to drink and dance. I'd order the most outrageous drink combinations. These combinations usually put me figuratively under the table, and once they literally put me under the table.

I was walking unsteadily from the women's restroom behind a mid-sized partition that hid my lower body. I waved to my sister and cousin, only to suddenly disappear. I'd dipped down and suddenly I was gone! My sister Margo peered over the wall and by then I was getting up. It was a ragged night; the toilet paper dispenser in the women's room was out of paper, and my sister used a glove she had in her purse. I am not proud to report these ignominious anecdotes about my crazy youth. My Mother wasn't happy with my drinking. And worst of all, when I returned from one of these not-so-secret debacles, she'd say with disgust, "You smell of man."

I don't recall that there was much "man smell" or any kind of female/male juices going on; we were still good Catholic girls, and if someone was loose in that way, she was a marked woman. It's hard to believe, but we really did just drink and dance. The good thing was that we traveled in packs, and the other thing was that sisters, cousins and other relatives were usually in the mix, and so if anything happened that was out of the ordinary—and it didn't—we would either watch out for or tattle on each other. I was never about to even make out with my sister or cousin in the car. Most often the girls all sat in the back fending off any unwanted interest as we smoked cigarettes and giggled to ourselves.

My sister Margo and I often hung out. Only thirteen months apart in age, we wore each other's clothing, or rather, I wore hers, and she was my caretaker on those Juárez jaunts. I was the one who always got caught, the one who had the blatant unbelievable excuses about why I was home at 3 a.m. I was the one who straggled in without a prayer. My Mother always said about my sister and me, "Your sister listens to me, says yes ma'am and then does as she pleases. And you, you—" she shook her head when she said this—"you always fight me and then you obey me."

Oh yeah? Most of the time, anyway.

We ate tacos and sandwiches in Juárez at Fred's, a popular sandwich place, to dispel our crudas early in the morning. Fred's was a place made famous by the college kids. Our homes away from home in those days were the joints where we imagined ourselves grown up and sophisticated: the Noa Noa Bar, the Caverns, the Kentucky Club. In those dimly lit bars and restaurants we plotted our escape from family.

I've eaten tacos in all physical and mental states and I have to say I am glad I don't drink so foolishly anymore. I don't recommend this behavior to anyone and feel sad to see young people drinking heavily for fun. And yet, I did it myself. I wish I could go back and alter the past. I wasted so much time doing silly things, loving the wrong people and not paying attention to the valuable people and things in my life. My Mother was always talking to me about "priorities," and I never understood her fully.

A taco can set you straight and help you move on to the basics, to the really important things.

Our life was full of sobritas, leftovers, so I recommend them to you.

There's nothing better than a taco de sobritas, leftover food. You'd be surprised what tastes good in good tortillas: leftover chicken, fideos (vermicelli with tomato sauce), even lettuce and tomato with chile. I used to be addicted to a taco with A1 sauce. My Father loved A1 sauce and so my Mother kept it around in the early days. I came to love it on a warm tortilla or on a piece of white bread.

Always keep either Masa Harina or another brand on hand to make your corn tortillas. Or keep a dozen or two or three of the best local tortillas in your refrigerator. There's nothing easier and tastier to make than a good quesadilla on a favorite sartén, any time, day or night. Our Thanksgiving and Christmas meals consisted of tacos. Tacos and lots of biscochos. Nothing better!

We never had turkey on Thanksgiving, not once. Maybe a small chicken found its way into the kitchen, but for the most part our festive food was tacos.

And they are good, day or night! In México and Europe it's not unusual to eat late at night. Since my husband is French, I've come to eat a late dinner, and I remember eating dinner in México City at two in the morning. It's all in what you are accustomed to.

I am not advocating eating late, merely stating the reality. As I'm someone who works best in the late afternoon and at night, sometimes my eating habits have been erratic. I'm trying to change this. Always keep corn tortillas and flour tortillas on hand. They are indispensable! And whatever you do, remember, moderation is the key. I should and I do know!

Comida de Casa/Homemade Food

We always had tortillas de harina on hand at home as well as a pot of beans either on the stove or in the refrigerator. Mother cooked her frijoles in her seasoned Mexican clay olla that she bought in Juárez at the Mercado Juárez, her favorite indoor market.

CONSEJO

The best way to cook your beans is in a Mexican clay olla that has been properly seasoned with salt, Sylvia Bejarano, a friend who works at the local Hertz Rent A Car, tells me. The pot contains a little bit of lime, and this seasons and softens the beans. The clay also adds a nice earthy flavor, says my editor, Susan Humphreys, and you can smell the pot itself as well as the beans. But first you have to cure the olla with salt. If you don't cook your beans in a clay olla, you need to cook them slowly. The best invention for beans lovers has been the Crock-Pot.

We never made tortillas de maíz a mano. My mother was first a traveling Spanish teacher and later taught third grade in the Las Cruces Public Schools. She didn't have time to make tortillas de maíz. We bought our fresh corn tortillas either from local tortillerías or at the Mercado Juárez from women who sold their kilos of soft, warm tortillas in the middle of the Mercado near the fruit and vegetable booths.

My sister and I often went to Juárez with our Mother. It was simpler to cross the border then. There were no pot-sniffing dogs, no Migra pullovers by nasty-looking brown-faced men who should know better, no racial profiling, no ugly comments or unpleasant vibrations, no declaring oneself tried and true. There was no fear.

Since my Mother worked as a teacher, she hired women of all ages to help us maintain our home and help with child care when we were young. There were ayudantes/helpers of all ages, some barely older than my teenage sister, some nearly as old as my grandmother. Some were single, some married, some were widows, and all of them came from México. Some were legal, most were not. They were wonderful, decent women, except for the woman who stole my Mother's wedding rings, the woman she had to track down to her home on a far-flung cerrito, a remote hillside, to rescue her rings.

As a result of the often-changing helper scene, and because of my Mother's nature and temperament—she was a human rights activist, a tireless worker for her people, all people—we often found ourselves in Juárez on the weekend with a load of used clothing, old appliances still in working order, children's toys, bedding and assorted miscellaneous items that Mother had gathered. We'd put everything in Mother's blue Toyota and head down the road with a car full of things to give away either to one of our helpers—Ninfa … Regina … Cuca I … Cuca II … or Emilia—or to their extended families. We usually had no trouble crossing. My Mother was a formidable figure and no one dared ask her for a mordida. Even the most hardened general or policía or federale backed down when she insisted her clothing must cross. I don't think she ever paid a mordida, not her! No one was ever bribed by La Señora Chávez. ¡Nunca, jamás!

My Mother's gifts were most welcome. I wish I had been old enough and a filmmaker to document those trips with my Mother, Delfina, to any number of colonias in Juárez. I have seen incredible poverty, dire conditions, houses with earthen floors, walls made of cardboard or tin cans, shacks without running water, one spigot of water for the entire neighborhood, and that spigot with a dead rat nearby. And always, inside, there was gratitude and a warm tortilla. Inside were tacos, people struggling and succeeding in being family, and it was there I ate, was nourished and politicized in the ways of brotherhood/sisterhood. It was there in those poor homes among proud and happy people that I learned what it is to be human.

Inside those cardboard shacks, between the tin walls made from coffee cans, was to be found the best food, the deepest laughter and a profound freedom of spirit.

My friend Ellen McCracken shared a memory of eating a delicious tortilla in a small Mexican village with a poor family. The family had nothing to offer but a "taco de sal," a tortilla sprinkled with salt. This is the recipe.

Un Taco de Sal

Take a warm tortilla de maíz.

If you have mantequilla/butter, spread it on the tortilla while it is hot.

If you don't have butter, sprinkle on a little bit of salt.

Enjoy the feast!

———

Living on the border between countries, one well off and one less so, it's easy to forget how difficult life can be on el otro lado, the other side.

The following recipe comes from a newspaper in Juárez. A woman in Anapra, a suburb and border crossing near Juárez, was stopped by Mexican officials and questioned about her frequent trips back and forth across the border in which she transported cases of American dog food. Was she selling it, they asked? She informed her interrogators that she had been buying American dog food for years to feed her family. According to her, American dog food was better than Mexican dog food because of its vitamins and nutrients. Also, American dog food really spread well, she added.

This recipe then, is for all those who have eaten or will eat dog food. For those of us who have never tried it, it's about time we did.

Dog Food Tacos

1 can dog food. I suggest you experiment with various brands.
You will eventually discern your favorites.

1 can opener

1 dozen warm tortillas, homemade, if possible

Open dog food.
Warm dog food over low fire, stirring often, or heat in microwave.
Warm tortilla on a comal or your favorite sartén.
Slather warm dog food on a warm tortilla.
¡Buen provecho! Mmmm!

No matter what side you are on, there is always another side. Another taco.

Tacos and Burritos: So Close and Yet So Far

What is the difference between a burrito and a taco? This is a very important question, and the answer is very subjective.

Tacos to me are more formal than burritos and have a hard, fried tortilla shell, unless of course, you have a soft fried taco. A burrito is softer, more thrown together, the informal cousin of the taco. In San Antonio, their tacos are my burritos, and in Wyoming, forget it: enchiladas are made with flour tortillas. So what is the difference between a burrito and a taco? Both have a filling inside, but one is wrapped in a flour tortilla, the other in a tortilla de maíz, but then again, what is the difference between a taco and a burrito? The answer is what culture is all about!

Tacos were and are special. They require time and commitment, and if possible, are best prepared with another person. It's better to roll together, especially if you have many dozens of tacos to make. I've made over twenty dozen tacos by myself at a given time. It was an enormous amount of work, but I wanted to give them to my Uncle Sammie for his wedding anniversary. It took several days to get everything together, but it made me happy to deliver the tacos to my uncle's house on the next street over. Everyone seemed surprised when I walked in with what seemed like never-ending trays of tacos. They were grateful to see them.

Let's get one thing straight: Mexican food takes a certain amount of time to cook. If you don't have the time, don't cook it. You can rush a Mexican meal, but you will pay in some way. You can buy so-called Mexican food at too many restaurants that say they cook Mexican food. But the real food, the most savory food, is prepared with time and love and at home. So, give up the illusion that you can throw Mexican food together. Just understand that you are going to have to make and take the time!

What Constitutes a Taco?

There are any number of things you can put in a tortilla and call a taco: eggs, potatoes, rice and beans, beans and rice, chile, asadero or cheese of any other kind, chiles rellenos, morcilla/blood sausage, any kind of meat, including lengua/tongue, cesos/brains, tripas/intestines, chicharrones/pork skins, barbacoa/barbecue, buche/cow gullet, chapulines/grasshoppers. And don't forget the fish: canned salmon, sardines, fish sticks. You name it, a tortilla can hold it.

My Mother loved to eat raw chile and would put a whole green chile inside a tortilla. We also ate tacos with baloney, potted meat, jam, Spam, chocolate, peanut butter and anything else that was in the refrigerator and tasted good.

There are endless permutations of what types of filling you can put in a tortilla. And yet, there's nothing better than a soft, warm, gently buttered tortilla to eat "as is." ¡Delicioso! ¡Una bendición!

An Expert in Taco-ology

I do not profess to be an expert in taco-ology, but by being a Mexicana and my Mother's daughter, I do understand tacos. We Mexicans know our food, or so we should.

As I travel around the United States, I have come to appreciate a really good taco, a superior tortilla, excellent rice and savory beans. Any deficiency in any area can make or break a restaurant. Gather a group of Mexicanos together and they will expound on the graces and vicissitudes of our food—abundance or lack, either of good Mexican food or the resources to prepare the food they remember.

I once spent a weekend in San Antonio, Texas, at a book festival there and ate most meals with a fellow writer, Benjamin Alire Sáenz. Both of us held forth on the San Anto tacos as we measured, evaluated and assessed the food. Ben swore that no one could ever hold a candle to his mother Eloisa's enchiladas. I retorted that my Mother Delfina's tacos were the world's best.

At one telling moment in a restaurant not to be named, reputedly a local legend, Ben squeezed a taco and out came Velveeta cheese. He was appalled. I didn't have the heart to confess to Ben that my Mother used Velveeta for her chile con queso.

My husband, Daniel, a lover of film, wished he'd had a camera along to "document" our food journey that long weekend as Ben and I traded quips about what we deemed inferior Mexican food.

I have since gone back to San Anto many times and believe the food is good; it could have been the combination of Ben and me, remembering the best of our mothers' incredible cuisine, food no one could duplicate, not here, not there, that caused us to be so harsh. I will say that San Antonio's tortillas are really good, some of the best to be found.

Replace the name of the town and you have other stories. For years I've begged people not to take me out to eat local comida Mexicana. Por favor. Begged is a strong word, but it's true. When I travel, I want Asian food, not Mexican. Funny about your hosts: some will appease my yen for Thai, Vietnamese or Japanese food, others just don't care, and others offer you a hearty meal at a joint generously donated by local raza. I am always grateful for a good taco, but please, let it be good. Good is subjective. Some of these off-the-beaten-track meals have been the best: chiles rellenos in a basement with an immigrant women's literacy group in New York City; homemade fideos and tacos in an elementary school gym in my hometown of Las Cruces; a tasty pork and guacamole burrito in the courtyard of a juvenile prison in Juárez; the best flauta I have ever eaten at El Rincón de las Flautas in Gómez Palacios, Durango, México.

As a lover of all ethnic foods, you have to be ready to eat wherever you are and whenever it is available. Once you can do that, all food becomes a blessing.

When I was in Chicago for a weeklong series of workshops with a local library, the organizers failed to note how the food was scheduled on a Friday. The young immigrant Latina girls were confounded and at a loss whether to eat the pepperoni pizza that sat invitingly on the tables. A cultural faux pas and how to remedy this? Remove the pepperoni and offer a prayer of thanks!

In our all-girls Catholic high school, called Madonna High School, where I was in a graduating class of twelve girls, appropriately called "The Apostellettes," we had a naïve but very strict Irish nun, Sister Leilia. When a group of the girls who boarded at the school went out to eat, they wanted to order hamburgers but Sister noted it was a Friday. My still-good friend Kathy Austin piped up gleefully, "Well then, let's order cheeseburgers." Sister did not catch on to Kathy's joke until later. The girls were heartily reprimanded.

Four of us Apostellettes still meet on a regular basis and laugh at Sister Leilia's foolishness and Kathy's inventiveness. This same Sister Leilia, for some reason, didn't like my younger sister, Margo. Maybe it was because she caught her going through a window at school to escape class and take off with her friends in a car during the school day. Whatever the reason, Sister Leilia, the school spiritual leader and counselor of Our Lady's Sodality, barred Margo from joining that society in praise of the Blessed Mother. What did Sister Leilia know about our culture, about tacos? If she had known more, she'd have been a kinder person.

What would have appeased that rigid, dour-faced Irish nun? A warm taco. Perhaps made by a Magdalene, the very short Mexican nuns who lived in a makeshift rundown, tumbledown series of shacks behind the elegant two-story building, the Convent of the Nuns of the Good Shepherd, where the upper-class nuns lived. Our Mother Superior, Mother Dominica, and an elite cadre of "teacher nuns" lived in the Big House in the middle of a large property, donated to the Good Shepherd nuns by whom? I am not sure. A few Irish, white, Filipina and maybe a token Mexican nun made it across the proverbial tracks into the main Mother House, but the Magdalenes lived in a perpetual state of penance in a ramshackle building behind the chapel.

There are Mexicans and there are Mexicans. And the Magdalenes were the lowest of the low. There were whispers that the Mexican nuns, las Magdalenas, were women who had formerly gone astray, had children out of wedlock, women who didn't have homes or families, or worse, had husbands who had left them. They deserved to live in the outlying, low-ceilinged dark addition to the side and back of the church. They didn't deserve to be seen: they were short, squat, dark-skinned, humble and simple women, puras indias.

They lived in their own area, ate their own food in their own space and were rarely seen. They were cloistered nuns, Kathy reports, and they wanted it that way. They were also penitents who believed in self-flagellation. We whispered among ourselves that if they really were "bad women," then they would just barely manage to save their souls by being nuns.

And yet now, as I look back on the inherent racism of that under-life of holiness, no man of any kind, no unwanted or wanted child, no broken or abusive home would be enough for me to beat myself the way I understand those nuns beat themselves in their search for salvation.

The Magdalenes were the worker bees of that sanctimonious hive, were the ones who cleaned up, cooked and presented us teenage girls with our beloved enchiladas or tacos on those celebratory occasions when they were served up and were most welcome. Sometimes these ciphers would feed us a meal—peanut butter in a hamburger or hot dog bun, Sloppy Joes on a corn tortilla. I remember eating a lot of hamburgers and peanut butter in high school.

Kathy remembers driving around town with Mr. Feather, a kind and elderly neighbor, who was a guardian angel to the nuns. Kathy would go to the grocery store with him, where they collected food donations: old fruit, passed-over vegetables, day-old bread, punched-in cans and outdated discards. Together they would sort through the best food and put it in his truck and drive the donated good food back to the convent, where the Magdalenas would use it to prepare their own meals as well as the meals of the Mother House and the students of Madonna High School.

I always had a feeling of oppression around those industrious, shadowy nuns. I now realize that this was learned behavior. Where did this racism come from if not the other nuns, the "good" nuns whose attitude we young women modeled and mirrored? The "good" nuns taught us to look at those poor women as "bad," and so we did. I never knew any one of them by name. Kathy only knew the name of one who caught her snooping around the Magdalenes' building out of curiosity and who got her in trouble. Kathy was forced to do penance by lying on the cold floor, face down, her arms in the shape of the cross.

It was proper the Magdalenes should be called just that. They were outcasts, like Mary Magdalene. They were like all of us young girls were then, women in bodies we weren't allowed to acknowledge.

I am your Mary Magdalene
come, let me wash your feet
stroke your brow
can we undo the past
throw it away
knotted cords of fevers, dreams

Often I have had to apologize
to men
for passions
wouldn't know
it would be this way

So, in high school
Johnny called to say:
you want too much
aren't you embarrassed, shy?

Discount the young boys
their chained libidos
their fat brothers
and forget those conversations
about how you are oversexed
and please, don't write me anymore

Okay, banishment—
that high tower
I can see all the way into the chambered heart
I am back at the place

overlooking blue land
surrounded by gargoyles
the wind

I am your Mary Magdalene
come, let me wash your feet

Throughout my lifetime, I have eaten enormous amounts of tacos, enchiladas, tamales, chiles rellenos, tostadas and salsa. Does that make me an expert? Yes, maybe so!

I've been fed by many women, all sorts of women, and to me, they were never "bad" or "good." They were merely women, working out their lives and destinies amongst the food and prayers. I don't profess to be an expert in living; all I know is that I like a good story, a great taco and to live among the truly free.

Botanas/Appetizers

¡Comida!

All my life I have worked in or around food. Before, during and after high
school, college and graduate school I was a waitress. I had plenty of time
to learn about Mexican food, its preparation and presentation, as well as
the high and low art of its cuisine. I worked mostly in Mexican restaurants, in a variety of well-known places, from Santa Fe to Las Cruces and
on to Dallas, Texas, and I learned much, not only about food but also about
people. I have worked beneath expensive chandeliers and wiped down

greasy plastic booths; I've served steaks and comida corriente/the daily special. I have waited on people of all ages and been stiffed by people of all nationalities. Thank God for waitress friends and kind bartenders who have helped me make up all the money I've lost from rude customers.

A lot of what I learned became the basis of my novel *Face of an Angel*, about a career waitress in a Mexican restaurant. It's not my life or my story, but what I saw slinging tacos contributed to the book. As a waitress, I have learned patience and sureness, openness and balance, intent and correctness. My greatest lesson has been to learn to flow with food, its preparation and cleanup. I loved waitressing and I was good at it. And I am proud to say I was selected by the head waitress, Carolyn Tarr, to train new waitresses at a Steak and Ale I worked at in Dallas, Texas, while I was completing my master's thesis, a play called *Mario and the Room María*. The play was set in an old hotel that had rooms named for women. The action of this intense family drama took place in a room called María.

Carolyn's vote of confidence in me meant so much! I worked the lunch shift and was out by mid-afternoon, when I returned home to watch the Dialing for Dollars movie, after which I would begin work on my thesis until dinnertime and sometimes afterward. Working as a waitress allowed me to leave my heavy theatrical world behind and just live in the moment. I had a great respect for my fellow waitresses that continues to this day. They were and are fine and strong women. I don't think I ever told Carolyn how much I respected and admired her. I have told Nellie, the head waitress at La Fonda Bar and Restaurant in Santa Fe, what she has meant to me. She was my mentor and role model for one incredible year as I struggled to find myself. Her even-tempered and professional manner taught me so much.

I've always appreciated food from in front of and behind the counter and from the kitchen to the dining room. I've been lucky to know tacos from the inside out. I have fallen in love near food, and food has consoled when the love has gone away.

I know food. And while I love food I know how hard it can be to work with food. I once sustained a concussion in a walk-in refrigerator when I bent down and then came up accidentally into a metal rack while refilling an enormous salad bowl. I once splattered hot steak juice on a suede jacket. I have sustained the rudeness of family and stranger alike. Hungry people are grouchy—we all know this—or they can be. I once had a woman apologize to me for being nasty. I was grateful for that apology and have come to realize that people are just people and not to take things said in a state of hunger personally. I have carried food out and brought it back. I've lifted trays and put them back on the shelf. I've worked so hard that at night my legs have flailed and twitched. I haven't slept at times, I was so tired, and I've also overslept, overeaten and slipped on salad dressing, wet lettuce and God knows what the hell was that, and I've known what food smells like on an unwashed uniform. And I have always appreciated the hard work food servers do.

I salute all waitresses, waiters, busboys and cooks. Where would we be without the nourishment of food? Food is necessary to fortify and replenish.

Bendiciones/blessings and a hearty thank you to all who work with food on a daily basis. Your work is important, it matters, it is the basis of all community.

COMIDA: A CREDO

I believe in food
the healing power of food
I believe all people, no matter what color, race or creed
no matter where they come from or who they are, should have food
nourishing food, hearty food, good food, food that sustains, empowers, trans-
    forms and heals
I believe all work is good
I believe all work is important

my work is my connection to all life
to all good
to all community
I believe in community

I believe in who I am
I believe in the work I do
I believe in myself
I believe in my sisters and brothers in work
We are family
I believe in family
creo en mi familia

I believe I am connected to my roots, mis raíces, to where I am and where I live
I believe that I belong to my time and my place
I know that there are all different types of families
To me they are all sacred
All nature, all life is my familia as well.
¡Gracias a mi familia!

Food of the People

It's good to be Mexican. Recently, at our Cultural Center de Mesilla, I visited with a man from California. He was admiring our collection of new books, books on the Southwest, books on Chicano and Latino culture, books in Spanish and English, bilingual children's books, books in Spanish for adults. In wonder, and with pride, he turned to me and said joyfully, "It's good to be Mexican!"

"Yes!" I agreed.

"The food, the music, the culture. It's good to be Mexican," he stated with delight. We both nodded.

"If I weren't Mexican," I added, "I would want to be Greek."

"Italian," he responded.

"Russian," I said remembering how in Russia, everyone said I was so "Georgian," their equivalent of "Latinos." For me, it was a great compliment to be called Georgian in spirit. On the trip, an exchange program of Americans and Russians called the Forum for U.S. and Soviet Dialogue, I had won the group award for the "person who hugged the most." It's a Mexican/Russian thing.

"God, it's good to be Mexican," the man repeated.

———•:•:•———

Nowadays, hoy en día, with our world full of war and violence and lack of love, a world full of greed, a world of domination, grasping power, venal stupidity, real evil, don't get me started, it's good to know that a conversation about tacos will always engender a sense of comfort and happiness. If only we could sit down at a big round world table and eat tacos in a spirit of love we might begin to work on world peace!

Stranger or kin, these are dangerous times to talk about war, affirmative action, immigration policies, the environment, the U.S. government, our president, and yet—a conversation about tacos always brings out first a smile, and then some sort of proclamation about any number of aspects of tacos, as well as advice and tips about either taco preparation or taco eating.

———•:•:•———

Last summer we offered a workshop called Tacos 101 at our Cultural Center. It was very successful and led to this book. Two summers ago we offered a workshop on the preparation of nopales/cactus pads. By understanding a people's food you can understand their culture and what they believe in. Our mission at the Cultural

Center de Mesilla is to bring understanding to people of all ages. We believe the knowledge and acceptance of many different cultures informs, enlightens and ultimately empowers us.

Located one block from the Mesilla Plaza, the Cultural Center was once home to a Mexican garrison and later, the well-known and loved D. C. Frietze grocery store, run by Mesilla's former mayor and his wife, our present landlords, Roberto and Eliza Frietze. The building is one of Mesilla's oldest adobes and is permeated with a sense of history and story that is at the heart of our Southwestern landscape. Our events have reached hundreds of people who have never come out before to support literature. We have reached rural communities in Mesilla, Vado, Chamberino, La Union, Anthony, Derry and elsewhere. A book signing for Rudolfo Anaya in December 2004 brought over four hundred people who waited for hours to have Mr. Anaya, the godfather of New Mexican literature, sign their books. We had scheduled a reading, but it was not possible because the line went down the street and past the acequia/irrigation ditch.

When we offered our nopal-cooking workshop, a local woman was stunned to learn that "nopalitos" were a food. There is a well-known local Mexican restaurant called Nopalitos in town, but she had never made the connection.

"Nopalitos? You mean it *means* something?" she said in a startled voice.

She knew about Nopalitos the restaurant and thought the story ended there.

"Nopalitos are the food of our desert people," I said.

The woman had no reckoning with nopalitos. Some might say, why should she? I need to say, why didn't she? The great wheel of learning and appreciating one's own and others' cultures is what makes us global citizens.

"Nopalitos, you mean it *means* something?" I will never forget the woman's surprise.

It is this lack of understanding about the basics of cultural life that have prompted us to inform, educate and empower our audiences through our work at the Cultural Center de Mesilla with our year-round workshops and literary and arts events programming for people of all ages, including workshops like Tacos 101, calavera/sugar-skull decorating workshops for Día de Los Muertos/Day of the Dead, as well as a tamalada/tamal-making workshop in collaboration with a local tortillería, Las Cruces Foods, Inc.

At the root of all our work is the core belief that cultural knowledge allows us to see our interconnectedness to each other, no matter what our backgrounds. The Cultural Center de Mesilla is a resource center and clearinghouse for the arts, as well as a place where community can find a way to understand itself.

Oftentimes I reflect on how someone can live in this desert place, so close to the Mexican border, and not feel some sense of appreciation for what is inherently of this place. I am not only talking of food, but also the language and customs. How long can a person live in a culture and be closed to it? Forever, if you wish. But why?

Diego Rivera and a Table Full of Shoes

My Mother, Delfina Rede Faver Chávez, studied Spanish for thirteen summers in México City in the 1930s and 1940s at the National University of México, UNAM. She was a student of Diego Rivera's in an art history class. She recalled a memorable night when the lights failed. Profesor Rivera taught the class by candlelight, a taper held under his chin, the candle's soft glow illuminating the now familiar features: the puffy face, large watery frog eyes, the fleshy lips.

"It was magical," Mother said, and for a moment I felt her love for all things Mexican—for its art, its culture, its food and the embodiment of lo Mexicano, her art history professor, Don Diego Rivera. I have no doubt Don Diego knew her by name as well. Mother would often visit Don Diego when he was painting. She loved to watch him work and often recalled his talent and skill. She became a personal friend and never tired of recalling what a masterful artist he was. She was forever touched by these summers in México, and I have no doubt that despite the loneliness of her years as a widow, she found great strength in the presence of this great man and in all art.

She also personally knew Dolores Del Río, the famous Mexican actress, who in certain ways reminded me of my Mother, both physically and because of her elegance and beauty. I believe she met Dolores Del Río through Don Diego and his circle of friends. So much of that time of my Mother's life is a closed book! I've often wished I had been more inquisitive about that time in her life but I was a foolish girl then, without what my Mother called "priorities." And sadly, my Mother was like all parents, relegated to the known, when in fact she was a great mystery, one I will never fully understand.

Delfina Rede Faver would have stood out in any crowd. She was a striking dark-haired young woman with a beautiful body, a high, firm bust, glorious and mysterious deep-set dark brown eyes, a woman vestida de luto, a still-young woman in her late twenties dressed all in black. She was in mourning for her young husband, Tiburcio "Bucho" Faver.

My Mother was untouchable then. Unattainable. Shrouded in glorious suffering. I like to imagine that this formidable but captivating young woman, who knew what she had to do and would let nothing stop her, rebuffed even the smooth-voiced Don Diego. She had a fatherless young daughter, and education was her balm and salvation, her hope of getting ahead.

It is from this woman that I have learned most of what I've needed to know in this world. She was never rich, never too poor, never too happy, maybe often too sad; she believed in the power of the mind and the compassion and mercy of the human heart; she was a bit of a romantic but not too much; life dealt her a memorable hard hand and she took it up and played it out. My Mother struggled to make ends meet, but that didn't stop her from always moving forward, looking well dressed, muy de moda. She always loved a good sale and counted on the occasional incredible buy to make her day.

There was once a giant closeout sale that took place at the Arcade Shoe Store on south Main Street. The store was inside our first mall, a building with a long walkway that sloped downward toward Main Street. As a child I thought it was great fun to go there and run up and down the enclosed building that was the only one of its type in all of Las Cruces.

It was at the Arcade Shoe Store where I yelled out, much to her embarrassment, "Mother, is size eleven too small?" She was shocked that I let everyone know her large shoe size.

It wasn't that her feet were so big, she said as if clarifying the situation, "It's that I have calluses and corns and have to wear extra-large shoes with support hose to help my bad varicose veins. And not only that, your voice carries!" she scolded me, wishing I weren't so loud and was a little more subtle.

I generally spoke what was on my mind and didn't care who heard. Now that I think of it, I was very much like her!

The Arcade Shoe Store was going out of business. The large signs said: Final Days! Giant Liquidation. Going Out of Business, Forever. This Is It!

Over several weeks the shoes went from full price to half price and then down to $10. Near the end of the sale, shoes were marked down to $1 a pair.

It wasn't surprising that my Mother, an inveterate shopper, came home with a hundred pairs of shoes, all priced a dollar. All were in boxes that showed the shoe size, style and color. The boxes faced the front door of the house, so that when you came into the living room you immediately saw the large, round dining room table that was filled with shoeboxes. This is the same table that served as Taco Central, where all festive meals were celebrated and enjoyed.

Shoeboxes were piled high on the floor as well and snaked their way into the living room. If anyone came into the house, and there was always someone coming into the house, he or she was invited to select a pair of shoes.

The large circular dining room table, our Taco Table, was occupied for months, as people made their way through the boxes. For a while all taco meals, all meals, were suspended or relegated to either the small 1950s vintage red and white spot-ted Formica kitchen table, set just so in a too-small kitchen (one centimeter off and you couldn't get into the laundry room), or to a TV tray in the Blue Room, which by this time had become the TV room, where my Mother's news programs held sway all hours of the day and night.

A well-read, intellectual woman, my Mother watched the early morning news, the noon news and the seven and ten o'clock news broadcasts. With the news as background, she got ready for her teaching duties, came home to get the mail, no child support check in sight, and wound down in the early evening in front of her much-used sewing machine, constructing a dress for my sister or me, or hemming one of her many tablecloths or handmade purses or pillows.

The late-night news found Mother dressed in her soft men's flannel pajamas, size XX, my old blue ballet class leg warmers over her pants bottoms—they helped her bad varicose-filled legs she said—as she sat, her long still-dark hair loose and shiny in front of the television, capturing the last flickering of world news of the day. Soon she would be headed off to sleep, only to begin again another day as a dutiful and loving teacher and Mother. As she passed me, she turned off all the lights, which meant only one thing: everyone and that included me, was to get to bed immediately. No late-night television watching. To bed, now! ¡Ya! Mother hummed an indescribable one-note tune I've never been able to replicate, but which I remember in my bones. It was a sad, haunting melody, and it always broke my heart to hear it.

Every morning there were those shoes that stared you in the face from the top of the Taco Table. Would they ever go away? The task of distributing a hundred pairs of shoes seemed daunting at first, but surprisingly, it was easier than anyone imagined.

Even my long-missing Father found a pair of shoes on the round table. He ribbed my Mother ruthlessly about the shoes and all her sales items, but I think he was secretly proud of her business acumen and ability to find a good deal any-where and at any time.

The shoes usurped all else. People would come over and rumble through all the boxes looking for their size and fit. It took constant attention to organize the boxes and redistribute the remaining shoes. I'm not sure anyone thought of arranging the boxes according to style or size. No time for that. In one area near the large window that faced out to the back yard and the vacant lot where the two neighbor boys played in a dugout fort, there were about five or six pairs of men's white loafers, comfy-looking nurse's type of shoes.

You didn't want to stand back there too much or you'd have to listen, especially in the summertime, to the two neighborhood boys, one younger, one older, bickering with each other. The older tortured and abused the younger, and the younger was a terrible whiner whose shrill cries echoed through the neighborhood. Their constant arguments were awful to hear. I never articulated my distress to anyone on hearing them carry on, although many years later I did inform my Mother about the two ugly brothers.

"Why didn't you tell me about them then?" she asked.

It was a yell-y neighborhood, and so many neighbors and family shouted to each other, I guess I didn't feel the need to let her know about the brothers. Who knows?

I remember I used to cover my ears to stop the noise of the younger one's sharp cries as the older brother pummeled him and yanked him around. I hated the young brother as much as the older, as he goaded his brother by screeching that he was going to tell.

"I'm going to tell Mama. Just hit me and I'll tell. I'll tell. Just hit me, go on, hit me! Aaaah!!!!"

Just tell someone, I silently begged, tell someone. Anyone. Just tell them and get it over with. I dreaded the summers.

The white loafers took hold in that space near the window where you could see all of the back yard and the vacant lot, and were probably some of the pairs that hung around the longest. Once I made a harsh comment to Mother about the white shoes, speculating that they wouldn't ever find feet to love them.

"Oh no," she said, in that voice of eternal optimism, "the shoes are already spoken for. Rosalinda's brother, Eduardo Quintanar, is in dental school in Torreón, México, and he's a size 10!"

Over a period of a month or so, all of the shoes and most of the boxes disappeared. Back then, I was a skeptical, critical girl, weary of my Mother's latest schemes and what I considered her well-intentioned but hare-brained plans. She always had something up that ingenious and generous sleeve of hers.

My Mother's kindness and generosity irritated me, as I felt she spent too much time giving to people who didn't really care about her and took advantage of her goodness. But it was more than that—it was the drama or "show" she always created—it was unnerving. Also, I was jealous of the time my Mother spent with others, time she should have spent with us when she was relaxed and calm, not the frantic, frenetic Mother time she gave us, all worry and care.

Yet Delfina Chávez never did anything carelessly, maliciously or without the underlying intention to do good. She was truly a fine woman and a decent man, and in that regard, she deserved the gifts we gave her for Father's Day. But as my Mother's girl child, I found her to be too strict, too hard, too embarrassing and too difficult to be around. She was much older than all my friends' parents, giving birth to me at age forty.

It was hard to live up to my Mother's expectations, to wear clean white gloves, clean white socks, clean white chones, to be a girl without stain or taint, any defect physical, spiritual or moral.

It was hard to roll a taco for my Mother as well. She once made me undo and re-roll several trays of abhorrent cara-outside tacos and tuck in that dark face that sadly greeted the world.

"How could you do that?" she demanded. "You know better!"

The shoes walked out of our lives. They were given as gifts, like the many identical cream-colored dresses with multicolored diagonal stripes she found at Aaronson Brothers Department Store on Main Street, all on sale. All the women relatives, and there were mostly girl cousins in our family, had one of those dresses, as well as the navy blue shift with the white cowl. My sister and I would inform each other before one or the other would decide to wear the multicolored dress or the navy blue shift. Sometimes we would show up to a family event and some unknowing prima, most likely LisaLilliaCharlotteHeleneBeverly, would turn up wearing the same dress. This was because my Aunt Elsie Chilton would hit the same sales as my Mother; often they traveled in packs together with another aunt, Lillian, who also loved a good buy.

The sisters-in-law ranged the aisles of Aaronson Brothers, the Popular, the United, the Budget Shop, and later, Bonanza City. Before the proliferation of dollar stores, my Mother and aunts were known to roam the streets of our small town in search of bargains. For special, once-in-a-while sales, they would cross the sacred portals of the better women's dress shops, Georjess or the Merry Go Round. But they only shopped there in the most exclusive women's shops when there was a sale.

Once my Mother forced me to plead with the owner of Georjess to reduce the price of some of the clothing in her sales racks. I was a shy girl and this begging mortified me. But I complied despite my horrified trepidation. I guess Mother figured if I were to ask the woman she would feel sorry for me: a skinny teenager with baggy clothes and bumpy skin. The woman, tall, stately and well dressed, peered down at me through her glasses and stated simply, "No, I can't do that. Everything's already on sale."

I slunk back to my Mother, who waited across the store, and told her we'd been refused. I think we left shortly afterward. And if we didn't, I probably went outside to get some fresh air. I couldn't tolerate my Mother using me the way she did, to bargain for things because I was a child. I hated it and she knew it. But it never stopped her from pulling out all the stops when she needed to. I find myself falling back on this learned behavior at times and it reminds me that I learned from a master. And yes, sometimes you have to create a scene, jump up and down, and stand up for whatever it is you believe in, whether it is justice or attempting to get a dress for a reduced price because you don't have the money.

My Mother and Aunt Elsie, both of them pinching that last dollar, that small over-extended dime, spread their budget thin with calculation, calculation, oh mighty, unmitigated calculation. They lived for the sales, that one special sale, that sale that superseded all the rest, that sale of a lifetime that would prove once and for all that they were wise buyers, good mothers, wonderful housekeepers, savvy businesswomen: by God they were not to be taken lightly, they knew who they were and they were good at what they did. That moment, that transitory, glorious moment, that sale, would be theirs, theirs!!

A Grito and a Song of Longing

¡Tacos! In general, most *Mexican* Mexicans are very cultured people, and this has nothing to do with formal education, wealth or titles. Mexican history and art are legendary, and the Spanish-language theatre to be found in México is some of the best in the world. Those of us who come from Mexican roots should know our Mother Country is a highly evolved place of industrious, talented and loving people.

I had a recent conversation with someone about the changing perception of Mexicanos and our culture. Many still see Mexican Americans and Mexican nationals through simplistic Frito Bandito imagery. We're either Mexicans slumped up against a nopal or beer-toting Cinco de Mayo party animals or a vato loco gang member.

First of all, no Mexicano in his right mind—and certainly no Mexicana—ever would be slumped up against a nopal with overhanging spiny pitayas that might fall down and stab you in the head! Someone invented this version of the lazy, mañana-centric peón who has nothing better to do than sleep next to a cactus!

Not enough people reflect deeply on the great culture that is México, with its highly evolved ancient cultures, architecture and art. What could be more amazing than the pyramids? And what is more beautiful than the music, the colors, the energy of this fiery, passionate world?

When I am in México, my husband says I become a different person—and I, too, believe something loosens and expands in me when I am on my ancestral turf. The joyous grito of my people comes bubbling up from inside me as I sing and then cry the beautiful and haunting lines from "Canción Mixteca" by José López Alavés that remind me of the passion, power and longing of my people, resounding affirmations of who I am and will always be, and how much home means to me:

CANCIÓN MIXTECA
YAA SAI SAU NUU MIXTECO
MIXTECAN SONG

¡Qué lejos estoy del suelo donde he nacido!
Ondè jícá cándee ri, jíín ñuù nù ní cacu rì
How far I am from the land where I was born

inmensa nostalgia invade mi pensamiento
xaàn ndávi táhàn ri, ja nácani inì rì
Immense sadness fills my thoughts

y al verme tan solo y triste cual hoja al viento
Chì máá un xinì rí, nátùhun un cuayo ndéché rí
To see myself so alone and so sad like a leaf in the wind

quisiera llorar, quisiera morir de sentimiento.

cuní rì ndehè rì, cuní rì cuù ri, uhù táhan rì.

I would like to cry, I would like to die from the feeling.

¡Oh tierra del sol, suspiro por verte!

Ñuù ndú ndícandíi, jacá nùu íní rì jahà rò

Oh! Land of the sun! I long to see you

ahora qué lejos yo vivo sin luz, sin amor

jà jícá cándee rì, tú cuti ndé jà cáhàn jiin rí

Now that I live so far from light and love

y al verme tan solo y triste cual hoja al viento

Chì máá un xinì rí, nátùhun un cuayo ndéché ri

To see myself so alone and so sad like a leaf in the wind.

quisiera llorar, quisiera morir de sentimiento.

cuní rì ndeherè ri, cuní rì cuù ri, uhù tahán rì.

I would like to cry, I would like to die from the feeling.

Among my Mother's greatest gifts to me were her Mexican-idad and her tacos.

Sopa Caldosa/Hot Soup

El Toque/The Touch

Besides my Mother's tacos, one of her best and most memorable dishes was her arroz. Try as I have all these years to make it, my rice can never equal hers. It was always fluffy, every single grain separated from the others. Seasoned with comino/cumin, it was never dry but always moist.

Some might call it Spanish rice, but this is a misnomer. I question the name Spanish rice. Where did the phrase "Spanish rice" come from?

Spanish rice is food racism at its not so subtlest. There's nothing Spanish about it except that people who speak Spanish make it. My Mother was a Mexican through and through. There is still no rice like hers; she had el toque, the touch. She tried to teach me how to make rice, but I never really learned. The recipe I've concocted is the closest I can get.

Delfina's Spanish—Really Mexican—Rice

1 small onion, diced

2 tablespoons cooking oil. I use canola oil, but my Mother used whatever leftover grease was in her tinita on top of the stove.

1 cup white rice. It's not necessary to have fancy, expensive health food rice, as I recall we never did.

1 cup juicy tomatoes, canned or fresh, chopped

2 cups hot water or broth

Comino/cumin to taste

Salt to taste

Sauté onions in a faithful sartén. Two tablespoons of oil should do it, but since onions vary, you will have to check, and you may need more. When the onions are soft, add rice. Add the cup of tomatoes. Stir gently and add 2 cups boiling or very hot water or broth. After the initial stirring of rice, tomatoes and water or broth, add the comino and salt, about a teaspoon each. After this, cover the rice and leave it alone. Don't look, don't touch and don't mess with the rice! Don't even think of looking at it until it is done. And how will you know when it is done?

You'll just know. Something in your body will start twitching and itching and you'll know, you'll just know it's ready. If for some reason you don't start twitching, it should take about 20 minutes. That is, if you use simple white rice and not brown rice. If you use brown rice, we know what kind of person you are, and it will take longer, about 45 minutes.

Take the rice from the heat and let it rest. If you are my Mother, your rice will be perfect. If you are like me, the rice will be pretty good, my husband's phrase for so-so or merely acceptable. His arbitrary "so-so" is what I fear my rice tastes like.

CONSEJO

The trick with rice really has to do with the process of sautéing the onion with the rice, browning the kernels a bit, and then gently adding in the tomato and spices, stirring the mixture with love and then leaving it alone. All my life I've fussed with rice. I don't know how to leave anything alone, especially food. Cooking Mexican food has taught me when to persist, when to let go; it has shown me which side goes in and which side goes out; and even more, it has given me the grace to know what is all right and what is better. I've learned from the best and finally I've allowed myself to step back and leave alone. Cooking comida Mexicana can teach even the hard-core impatient a benign patience.

Mexican—Not Spanish—Rice

Mexicans can never make Spanish rice; they can only make Mexican rice. Mexicans can make arroz al estilo Español but really what they make best is their own rice. Many people won't admit to being Mexican. They consider themselves Spanish. What can I say? This has led to a confusion of rice among other things. As for me, I consider myself a Mexicana/Mexican American/Chicana. So what kind of rice do I make? Let's not get lost in semantics or nationalism. And yet, let us celebrate who we really are. The questions and answers that lead to the discovery of self are to be found in one's true Culture.

We were all Mexicans on my Mother's side of my family. My Father had illusions of grandeur like many people from that time and place. They were this way because they had been beaten and worn down by poverty and racism, by tremendous lack and its opposite, grasping. They wanted more and got less, and never had enough money to hold on to the land they once owned, out in the hills of Doña Ana. They were people whose shame shamed them, but they couldn't articulate their anger. And as a result, they felt inferior. And as a result of their sense of inferiority, they became deracinated. It isn't easy for me to speak about this. I didn't know my ancestors' deprivation, their hunger or their want. All I know is that in searching for their American dream they forgot who they were. And in the forgetting, they moved away from language and culture.

I once asked my Father what his ethnicity was. He told me without hesitation that he was a "Spanish white man." My Mother, along with the rest of us, alas, was Mexican. And even worse than being a Mexican, my Mother was a Texan. I don't think my Father ever forgave her for her overweening sense of pride in being from over there, that other place, Texas.

This, then, was the great tragedy of my parents' lives, the fact that they were divorced not only in spirit, but in culture and core ethnicity. My Father would never admit to being a Mexican married to a Mexican.

The distinction between Spanish and Mexican is a sore point in our broken, unspoken-about New Mexico that few care to think about, with its racism and divisions between Spanish and Mexican. Northern New Mexicans consider themselves Spanish, while many of us who live in the south consider ourselves Mexican. There are always those who want nothing to do with the country of most of our ancestors. There exists an invisible membrane of denial for so many. The Spanish look down on the Mexicans, who sometimes look down on the Native American nativos. Many who have Mexican raíces/roots sometimes believe they are lesser than others—the way anyone who has been treated badly is made to feel lesser. And when you think you are nothing, you oppress others, whether it is other people, other cultures or your own family.

I have always been happy to say that my roots are from México. And in that pride comes an open honesty about who I am.

One of the least prejudiced people I've ever known was my Mother. And one of the most prejudiced was my Father. The only person who was more prejudiced than my Father was his mother, Lupe Triviz Chávez. Granma Lupe. Where she got this hatred of the Other, I will never know. I can only attribute this lack of compassion and acceptance to their hard lives, to the time in which they grew up and their reaction to their own displacement and mistreatment by Others.

My Mother often took Granma Lupe to the Fiesta Drive-In to see movies. She rued the day she took her to see the movie *Guess Who's Coming to Dinner?* with Sidney Poitier, who played the role of the fiancé of a beautiful white woman. "¿Pero cómo?" my Grandmother huffed. "Ay, ¿pero cómo? ¡No es posible!" Granma never recovered from this sacrilege of a movie with its impossible scenario.

My Father's family was afraid of black and Chinese people and anyone who wasn't a Spanish white person. My Mother and her people were respectful to Anglos; they spoke to them and about them in hushed tones, and with deference. They counted many Anglos as friends, something my Father's people did as well. If the Chávez could have, I think they would have chosen to be Anglo. And because of this estrangement from culture, I could never get a handle on who they imagined they were. I try to understand, but I don't. Both families were punished for speaking Spanish in the schoolyard. How is it that my Mother's family was even poorer than my Father's, more beset upon, and yet rose above their circumstances to embrace difference while my Father's family didn't? How is it that one family lost its culture and the other retained it?

When in Paris

When in Paris, France, don't buy tacos. You can eat them at home if you fix them yourself, but stay away from Mexican restaurants in Paris. Tacos, to me, are always a bargain, or should be, unless of course you're in France. In Paris I understand people pay $40 for a plate of tacos. If you are paying that much, something is definitely wrong.

Some of my best taco meals have been free or very inexpensive and were to be found in the homes of people who had little. There was always a hot tortilla waiting for us at Compadre Joe's house.

José "Joe" García was the neighborhood handyman who attended to all the neighborhood's needs. He was a handsome, dark-skinned Mexicano who had no formal training or license in anything other than making do. Compadre Joe was an expert in plumbing, electrical work, building and maintenance skills. He could as easily build a beautiful fountain out of Mexican tile as fix the moldy and corroded swamp cooler. Also, he had a lot of children. He was an expert in that as well. When he left his common-law wife for some disgraceful cuchispete, some nameless hussy, it was my Mother who brought them back together.

Little did Compadre Joe know that his wife and family would eventually leave him and move to the state of Utah.

"Utah?" I asked my Mother with surprise on hearing El Compadre had been abandoned after all these years by his rabble of needy kids and his now-legal wife.

"Yes, one of the girls lives there. They just decided to move."

A short, attractive man with the burnished dark skin of an Aztec god, he looked as if he'd walked out of an ancient legend. But no, Compadre Joe was always neatly dressed in a white short-sleeved shirt and dark pants. And not only that, although he had just a simple education back in México, he knew more about fixing things than my Father ever did. There was nothing El Compadre couldn't do. If he didn't know how to do something, which was rare, he'd wing it.

I remember him up high, standing on a ladder in my Mother's blue kitchen, fixing a light fixture, or walking gingerly and unafraid on our slanted roof as he drained water from the swamp cooler. We finally got an air conditioner when I was in college. Prior to this we only had several small window units in the living room and my Mother's bedroom. We used small fans and moved them around the house, depending on who and what needed to be cooled. In the 100-degree-plus summertime, my Mother, my sister Margo and I slept near an open window. Mother slept naked and liked to tell people unashamedly that she also did her house cleaning in the nude.

I don't know when that would have been, maybe in her later years when she lived alone, for when we were in school and living at home, the only place she was nude was in the privacy of her bedroom. Her head lay at the foot of the bed while her feet faced the headboard. Mother slept with a cold toalla on her forehead. The wet towel was her signature prop, and whenever we left the house for a trip in the car during the summer, she always gave us a wet washrag with which to cool ourselves. A plastic bag would keep the towel moist, and everyone was responsible for wetting his or her personal towel from time to time. During the unbearable summer heat, we all slept with a cold washrag nearby, to swab ourselves during the night.

I was a steamy adolescent, and Mother found me one morning with that once-wet towel between my legs. I don't think she wanted to think about what she thought I was thinking about. Not that I was thinking about that. In those days, sex was remote and unthought of. ¡Ay! But something had to be done, or so she imagined, to prevent any further problems.

Mother lectured me, but not too much. What she did was worse. She made me sleep with her for a number of days, making sure nothing happened with that onerous little rag. It was a horrible time. I was embarrassed, especially since I didn't think or couldn't remember if I really used the washrag the way she thought I had. And if I had, what business was it of hers? Especially since she slept in the nude, or so she said.

I'd been asleep when the unspeakable was supposed to have happened. How could I be punished for something I honestly couldn't remember?

Yet there was something comforting about the whole episode, as awful as it was: the two of us sleeping in homemade white cotton nightgowns, size XX, my Mother's trademark contribution to discreet yet comfortable sleepwear, our heads at the foot of the bed, both of us facing her pristine alabaster-colored wooden headboard. We faced a large crucifix on top of which hung askew a life-sized crown of real thorns over Christ's bleeding head. The little blue fan wheezed and sliced the air, but there was no relief for either of us in those hot, man-less summer days, those interminable and lonely nights.

———·•◦•·———

Life was never easy with my Mother. I felt she found countless ways to embarrass and humiliate me. I often wished she wasn't so tenderhearted and so kind. She was always crying and at so many inopportune times: joyful times, sad times, confused times, normal times.

She was civic-minded, caring about the least important person, and as a result of this, we were always going out of our way to help strangers. She helped drunks come in from the cold; she picked up hitchhikers at all hours of the day and night; she brought strangers home to stay with us. There were too many old ladies in our lives and we were always visiting one nun or another. If she wasn't helping someone pay their rent or utility bills, she was helping those who were living together get married. All of this took precious time!

My Mother's goodness was bothersome to me, a spoiled, restless girl. And now, in retrospect, I wouldn't trade for anything those days of wandering the streets and cerritos of Juárez with my over-zealous Mother as we carried seemingly endless bags of used clothing up little hills and inside dark houses.

"Señora Chávez, ¿no quiere unos tacos?"

"No, no tengo tiempo. Bueno, nomás una calientita …"

We knew what that meant. That one hot tortilla leading to another and then another. The food was good: savory tacos de res, frijoles refritos, whatever was there and at hand, sometimes only a hot freshly made tortilla de maíz con mantequilla, sweet cream butter, or spicy green strips of chile or queso Menonita that you bought at the Mercado Juárez on Diez y Seis de Septiembre Street, or at the Mercado Cuauhté-moc, which was behind and to the side of La Basilica de Nuestra Señora de Guadalupe, full of its Santería items, its horseshoe amulets for good luck in business and work, or pouches of El Polvo Legítimo contra la maldad, negro y blanco.

You had to cover all the bases, and the powders protected you against both black and white magic. The long-lasting, greasy-looking votive candles to El Niño Fidencio and Changó helped in different ways from the more traditional velas to La Virgen de Guadalupe and El Sagrado Corazón. It was good to leave no spiritual stone unturned, so a chicken foot might assist, or an Ojo de Dios, to ward off the evil eye, or maybe a swatch of aloe vera tied with red ribbon and the Miraculous Horseshoe that would cure that persistent stye and bring healing to those who refused to or didn't care to really see.

I loved Mercado Cuauhtémoc and maybe that's why my Mother didn't go there often. She was a more traditional woman, and what she needed to find she found at Mercado Juárez: handmade rebozos, long cotton dresses with colorful stitching, her beloved dulce de camote, her favorite candied sweet potato, and mine, the yellow, too sweet biznaga, made from barrel cactus.

We bought the asadero cheese or queso Menonita from a vendor near the front door and carried it to the center of the Mercado, where we bought a kilo of tortillas de maíz, still warm, that we carried outside to the car to eat.

You could tell the Mennonites in the Mercado by their simple garb, their straw hats, their funny little mustaches and strangely placed facial hair, their pale skin, and by the fact that their Spanish was a little shaky. The men wore simple, clean-looking clothing and spoke in halting jerky phrases, and the women were plain looking, self assured and unafraid to greet the day without any makeup or allure.

The tortillas at the Mercado were always good. We bought them in the center aisle from short, wrinkly viejitas who wrapped the still-warm kilo in cream-colored butcher paper that softened and expanded and held its savory charges, exuding a smell of earth and corn. The tortillas were to be eaten hot. Sin nada. Without anything. And they didn't need anything!

But if you had some freshly made asadero, the delicious homemade cheese, the tacos made with it were indescribable. And sometimes we bought the morcilla/blood sausage that was sold in large steaming pots as it cooked on a slow fire near the tortillas. I knew the sausage was made from blood, but I didn't care. Morcilla con una tortilla calientita—¡ay, que rico es la comida de mi gente!

Mother never allowed us to sit at the metal tables in the patio of the mercado, where patrons sat ordering food. Maybe she was afraid she would be hustled to buy the latest cassettes of popular Mexican singers, or any number of chucherías, things we couldn't afford, mugres that of course we longed for.

We sat in the dry heat of our car with nothing to drink as we ate our improvised tacos. Finally we would emerge, satiated and ready to shop some more. There was something so satisfying about eating a hot tortilla in the middle of the day, legs dangling out of a parked car, nothing better to do than enjoy the delicious perfection of a really great tortilla. There was nothing sweeter, more perfect, more pleasant, than to be unhurried and content with a still-warm tortilla and a simple hunk of cheese.

We re-entered the mercado and might head to the vegetable section, where Mother carefully selected ripe mangos. Out we'd go again to the car, as we slurped and sucked the incredibly sweet juice from those perfect mangos. We never ate them all and smuggled the last few home, safely tucked under the car seat.

Years later, when I mentioned smuggling mangos to a student of mine, Juan Gómez, a retired Border Patrol agent from McAllen, Texas, he couldn't get over my blatant admission that for over forty-five years I had brazenly smuggled hundreds of mangos across the border under the car seat. "Why did you do that? It's like sneaking a tortilla across the border!" Juan couldn't understand the absolute absurdity of my many food-smuggling transgressions. I might have told him that a smuggled mango tastes better than a declared mango. Nowadays mangos are acceptable fruit and can be crossed over without any problem. But then a mango was a delicacy, especially if it was rogue fruit!

Our stateside mangos are not the same as Mexican mangos. Mangos are also properly ripened in México, not like their hardened U.S. counterparts without flavor or color. Nor are U.S. tortillas the same as Mexican tortillas. It has to do with the flour and the way it is processed. Food is not the same food in different countries. If Juan didn't understand then, how can I explain it now?

MERCADO DAY

Mercado Day
Mango Day
Asadero Day
Blood Sausage Day

We sit in the car
Doors opened
Hanging out of seats
Peeling skin of mango fruit
Joyous
Without words
Eating

Mother in front
Father in back
Me at the wheel
We just finished our lunch
Asadero

Blood sausage
Avocados
¿Cuales están listas?
Tortillas de maíz
Las de deveras

Shivering dripping hands
Lift orange Fantas, Sprites and ice-cold Cokes
From the dispenser in the center aisle
Paid mariachis serenade us
With Guadalajara
Tierra quemada
As the shoeshine boys
With their shiny wooden boxes
Perch on the stairway
Watching us eat

Wet sticky hands
Cannot wipe away
The traces
Of this last holy meal
The parking lot
Receptacle of our remains

I drive through Juárez
Confident
Safe
I understand the way Mexicanos drive
They drive like me

I am not afraid
It is when I leave
The terror begins

Mercado Day
Mango Day
Asadero Day
Blood Sausage Day

I recalled that feast
Later in the rain

Mother is dead
My Father will never drive again

I step on the gas
I'm not afraid
I understand the way Mexicanos drive
They drive like me
Joyous
Singing
Guadalajara
Tierra quemada

¡Aguacates!
¡Queso fresco!
Dulces de camote
Mother's favorites
Los míos de biznaga

Señorita, por favor, algo para la familia
Ssst! Hey lady!
You want to buy?

Después
Later
Later I say

Mercado Day
Mango Day
Asadero Day
Blood Sausage Day

I recalled that feast
Later in the rain

The Nun's Diary

In my mind, my sane adult mind—the all-seeing eye of middle age—the greatest tragedy and most significant event of my childhood was my parents' divorce. At age ten I was the one who answered the door when the divorce papers were delivered. I was the one who handed the papers to my Mother. I remember the shock of it all—the howl that escaped from her body, how she wept hard, horrible tears and dragged herself through the house screaming. For a while she lay on the bathroom floor while my sister and I tried to revive her. Ay, ay, she wailed and then blacked out again.

This can't be happening, I thought. This can't be happening! But it was. While I was terribly sad and upset, I still remember thinking how very callous, rude and downright unforgivable it was for Daddy not to tell us he was leaving. But that was his style: to leave in the middle of the night, to slink out with the alcohol on his breath with promises to return. He was shiftless, irresponsible, not to be believed, an alcoholic womanizer.

When I think back now, I wonder if indeed this was the most significant event of my youth, after all. Oh, surely it was significant, but it wasn't crippling. After a while I adjusted. And besides, Daddy never really left us; he came back home on birthdays, Thanksgiving and Christmas. He came home, maybe or maybe not stayed with us, maybe or maybe not called us and invited us out to eat chicken-fried steak at the Town House Restaurant on north Main Street, or tasty juicy hamburgers at the Princess Drive-In, or to a movie at the Río Grande Theatre, or to a carnival in Mesilla. We met him at my Aunt Elsie's, which became for us a safe house. If he called, we would run over there, a block away, wildly, madly, excitedly, and he would often have gifts for us: pints of chocolate milk, pecan rolls from Stuckey's and bags of Beer Nuts. He was our illusive wastrel father, the unreliable bane of my Mother's sad existence, the great love of her life, and to us all he was the world and we never ever stopped loving him.

We recovered. I recovered. What maybe impacted me more as a young girl was the crushing loneliness I always felt. My aloneness. No one understood me. I had no one to talk to. I was small and skinny. I wasn't popular. My clothes didn't fit me. Mother made my clothes, and I thought they were ugly. Baby doll clothes, nothing sophisticated. And not only that, but Mother was older than anyone else's mother. She was out of step and severe. She didn't play with us, never knew how to play. Nor did I want to play with her. She was older, her breasts were too large. She was always talking about my Father. She knew he would come back someday. She was a religious fanatic, and her constant prayers tired me. I always questioned God and the Catholic Church. I was afraid of nuns, disliked priests. Mother went to Mass early every morning. She wanted me to be a nun. I just wanted to leave home, get away, and as soon as possible. I had no one to talk to, no one understood me, and I was alone. This is when I began to write in my diary. This is when I realized I was a writer and that writing would always be a way to look at my life, understand it and begin to heal it. I would write about who I was, my family.

I'm still writing.

The last time I saw Father
Everything surrounding him was borrowed
The plaza bench from some old man
Who sat there Sundays
His wife at the time
Who was always assigning possession to things
My meat loaf
My, my, my
My
Apartment, where the neighborhood kid
Dug holes in the lawn, there was no lawn
At that time
There were breaths, coughs

He drank himself sick whenever he could
And sometimes, his wife joined him,
Sadly, on benches, to rest

Sopa Seca/Rice or Pasta

Every City's Tacos

Every city has its tacos. There is always a good place to eat in any city, if only you can find it. Sometimes it's a well-known restaurant, oftentimes it's not. Sometimes it's someone's home—more often than not, it's someone's home.

My husband, Daniel, still talks about the mole we had in Houston over ten years ago at Walter and Yolanda Birdwell's house. Yolanda's mother was from México. She made an indescribable mole and also gave me a delantal/an apron I wore on stage during a reading. That mole was one of the best I've ever eaten. Like the French, who recall meals from years before, I remember many tortillas and many tacos. But of all the tacos I've had, I remember my Mother's the most.

Who can't remember a certain food, the story of that food, the night or day of that food, the story of the people you ate the food with and what you felt?

Every city has its tacos.

In Santa Barbara, California, you should try the tacos de rajas con queso at a restaurant called Los Arroyos. The rajas, slices of roasted chile, are sautéed with onion and seasoning. Ay, I have to echar un grito when I think of those tacos.

As far as tacos go, you have to start with a good tortilla. I've had many good tortillas in many different places. San Antonio, Texas, is a good place for tortillas, la pura tortilla. Pricey restaurants don't necessarily assure you a good tortilla.

Besides the tortilla, the filling has to be good—halibut at the Paradise Café in Santa Barbara, blood sausage at the Mercado Juárez, maybe fried baloney at home. I grew up on potted meat and Vienna sausage, occasional Spam and corned beef hash, canned salmon, tuna de vez en cuando. You threw what you had in the refrigerator into a tortilla.

I remember my older sister, Faride, telling me that once she'd eaten one of Mother's tacos and felt they were the best she'd ever had. When she asked what was different, Mother had told her she'd put some leftover potato salad in the meat.

We always had tortillas de harina on hand that my Mother made from white flour, as well as corn tortillas from the local tortillería. My sister's best friend's father, Mike Grijalva, owned a tortillería and we were familiar with his brand, Las Cruces Foods, Inc. At an early age, we knew tortillas, which ones to choose, which ones to avoid.

CONSEJO

Never select thin, doughy looking tortillas for rolled tacos. Select the thicker, hardier looking ones. For enchiladas, get the thick tortillas as well; they are tastier. Sometimes the tortillas will disintegrate into a mush if they are too thin. This isn't bad after a few days of reheating enchiladas, but in the beginning you want a substantial tortilla.

———•◦•◦•———

We take tacos for granted. A good lesson in gratitude is to buy a bag of Masa Harina or Maseca, the instant corn masa mixes, or the pura masa at your local tortillería, and make some homemade tortillas. You will begin to value the care and work that goes into making a tortilla. We take our corn so much for granted as well. Nor do we esteem the women who make tortillas a mano. And we especially denigrate the people who harvest and bring that food to us.

Soft Meat Tacos

I ate soft meat tacos when I was a little girl, in gently fried tortillas, "the little kids' way," a way I still enjoy. The little kids and the older people ate tacos this way at our house. The harder, rolled tacos with cheese or the semi-hard rolled tacos in the sartén were for all the others, people who could chew, who still had teeth and didn't have trouble swallowing. People were either in the hard or soft taco category and this depended on age, health and swallow-ability.

Granma Lupe and Mamá Toña, my two aged grandmothers, never even got little kids' tacos; they were given watery taco meat in a small dish. Any number of older and younger kids could be seen eating these soft tacos. In his early fifties my Father began to have trouble swallowing, and as he got older, he came to depend on little kids' tacos or the Pasta that he so loved. Pasta in our family was not pasta. It was never an Italian dish, but a version of mincemeat my grandmother, Guadalupe "Lupe" Triviz Chávez, perfected.

I make Granma Lupe's Pasta often, and people are glad to see it come their way. Other than me, I don't know anyone in the Chávez family who still makes it. I have shared my Aunt Elsie's recipe with various cousins and my sisters, but they aren't interested in making it. My younger sister admitted to me recently that she hasn't made tacos in years. Years?? What's wrong with you? I thought.

Highly valued and much loved, Granma Lupe's Pasta was made for special occasions, especially during Thanksgiving and Christmas. My Mother learned to make it to please my Father, who was always visiting us and eating meals with us despite the fact my parents had been long divorced. As long as she could, my Mother held my Father tight in her embrace, and one of her many hooks was her irrefutably wonderful Pasta.

Granma Lupe's Pasta

This recipe was given to me by my Aunt Elsie Chávez Chilton. It is a Chávez family favorite, served on special occasions, sadly not so often anymore, as few people have the recipe and either don't have the time to make it or don't care enough about it. I never really appreciated it until I started making it.

2 celery stalks, diced

1 small onion, diced

1 cup raisins

3 small apples, diced

1 pound of hamburger meat

½ cup sugar

½ cup brown sugar

½ cup pecans

Dash of allspice

Dash of salt

1 bouillon cube or meat or vegetable broth

Water, as needed

Steam or boil celery, onion, raisins and apples until tender. I prefer steaming; it's better. Cook and drain the hamburger meat. Dump all together with the celery, onion, raisin and apple mixture. These are Aunt Elsie's instructions, not mine.

Add regular sugar. Add brown sugar. You might try using piloncillo, flaking the brown sugar cone for a rich flavor. Add pecans. Simmer all ingredients on a low fire for a long time.

Add a dash of allspice or pumpkin pie spice. Add a dash of salt. Add a bouillon cube or meat broth. I use vegetable broth. Add water as needed.

Keep stirring until done—a long time—until the Pasta takes on a "caca" color. Again, this is Aunt Elsie's quote. So don't blame me!

The Pasta can be used in tacos or empanadas or it can be eaten alone. It is a wonderful filling, much like mincemeat.

I recently met someone who also had something like the Chávez Pasta in their family. I can't remember who it was, so if you read this recipe, please contact me. I have no idea where this word comes from in the context of this dish so if you know anything, please let me know. We have a lot to talk about.

The Two Grandmothers

Granma Lupe was wheelchair-bound for over thirty years and lived with my Aunt Elsie. Her small room was off the kitchen, my aunt's washer and dryer to one side. It was Granma Lupe's job to fold the clothing for a family of ten. Her small twin bed was positioned in one corner of the room, across from a low brick bookshelf that held all her worldly possessions. Dried-out palms from Palm Sunday were casually draped over her children's photographs: her dead son Alejandro in his World War II uniform, my Father looking lawyer-ly, his hand on a large black book. Photographs of myriad buck-toothed and goofy-eyed grandchildren were placed on the wall above and around the bookshelf. On the two wooden shelves were boxes of unopened, crisply pressed linen handkerchiefs, assorted Christmas tea towels, enormous frilly birthday and Valentine's cards, imprinted holy cards with the date of death of too many relatives and ragged, dog-eared images of Our Lady of Guadalupe in her full regalia and the Sacred Heart with gleaming rays of gold pouring out from his opened chest cavity. Granma Lupe lived in this small precious world, and she seemed content.

My other grandmother, Mamá Toña, my Mother's mother, a fragile woman in her eighties, visited us in the summers. She was a retired postmistress from Redford, Texas, who was now living with my Aunt Chita in the dusty hinterlands of unbelievably Far West Texas. Her hobby was sewing. My Mother often gave her projects like stitching a red border on limpiadores, the homemade white kitchen towels we always used. Mamá Toña had already sewn her initials, A.R., for Antonia Rede, into all her personal clothing.

Mamá Toña's sister, a tiny hunchbacked woman named Manina, later came to live with us at our house in Las Cruces. She was very old and somehow it was decided my Mother would take care of her. Manina liked to play the piano, and early on during her time with us, when getting up from the piano after playing a tune, she fell down and broke her hip. Less than a year later she died in our house.

So much has changed over the years. Granma Lupe, Mamá Toña, Manina and my rascal father, the inimitable Mr. C., once all sat around my Mother's round Taco Table at one time or another and ate little kids' tacos. They are all dead now.

Despierta, mi bien, despierta,

Mira que ya amaneció,

Ya los pajaritos cantan,
La luna ya se metió.

A Family of Feet

My Father and I always had a close connection to each other, as we were born under the sign of Leo one week apart, in the late August heat. We were also the only ones in our family who had arches, and in our flat-footed clan we were the celebrated ones.

I am a chosen one. I have arches. This in itself makes me special. Much is expected of me, and of my feet. Everyone in our family views flat feet as a curse, an anathema and a symbol of imperfection. My Mother viewed flat feet as a stigma.

"You're the lucky one," she used to say. "Your feet aren't flat. You have an arch. Only you and your Father have an arch in this family. The rest of us, me, your sisters, we have flat feet. All my life I wished I had an arch. It's caused me a lot of pain, not having an arch. And not only that, your feet are small. The rest of us have huge flat feet. You're lucky. The only thing I gave you was your long second toe, the Rede toe. It was your Grandmother's toe, it's my toe, and now, it's your toe."

I considered having the infamous "Rede toe" an aberration of nature. It was ugly and caused my otherwise perfect feet to feel deformed. While all my friends and cousins had toes that graduated in size from the largest to the smallest, my second toe was longer than the big toe, and not only that, I felt it was hammer-headed, with a bulbous tip.

Feeling ugly-toed, I tormented my younger sister, who was doubly cursed with her bumpy, bulgy Rede toes and pale, flat-as-a-pancake feet. I mercilessly made fun of her hooked toes. It was only years later that I came to understand this condition as "Morton's toe." It causes the Morton-toed person to have a permanent callus radiating downward behind the toe toward the heel, and not only that, it causes some kind of shifting compensation when you walk. I didn't know it then. All I knew was that even though I was among the chosen few to have an arch in a splay-footed family, I was still singled out by the foot god to be Morton-toed. Having the condition as a child was a distressing and awkward thing for me. Whenever I was in public, I hid my feet. Those few times anyone looked at my feet in sandals, I quickly moved away. I consoled myself with the fact that I had an arch. And having an arch was a precious thing.

I remember going swimming with my younger sister, Margo, at my Uncle Sammie's house during the summer. I taunted her, saying she had long skinny banana feet. It was cruel. I made imprints of my perfect arch with pool water on the hot concrete and challenged her to make arches like mine. Twisting her foot sideways and rolling it across the concrete quickly, before it dried in the 100-degree heat, she would try to match my arch, molding her foot to what my Mother deemed perfection. She managed to create an artificial arch, and if you didn't know otherwise and if you saw her footprints on the hot concrete, you might think she was arch blessed. I remember my sister turning this way and that, imprinting her fake arch as best she could before the sun dried out her handiwork. I stood by, arrogantly nonchalant, feeling my arch-gifted feet superior.

I was brought up to believe that my gift was a sign of my eventual success. In what I wasn't really sure. All I knew was that somehow I had been singled out by fate to have an arch, a sign of great blessings, a sign that I wouldn't have to suffer the fate of my Mother, with her purple legs, her scarred, stripped veins, her always-throbbing feet. I just knew her fate would escape me. She was a teacher, and I never wanted to be a teacher. I was created for greater things, a life of more comfort, less sorrow. My parents were divorced, and I knew I would never divorce. I would never have to wait like my Mother did for the child support check that never came, the occasional fifty dollars that would mean so much. I wouldn't have to sit in front of a small wooden desk late at night like my Mother did, figuring out what bills to pay, struggling with a ledger that never balanced out. The irony is that I have played out this same scenario too many times. And each time I sit hunched over my bills at a small desk in an over-heated room, I see my Mother in front of me, weighing her options.

My life would be different, I promised myself. My feet would take me far from my Mother's life, her constant anxieties, her brutal and all-too-real battles. I wouldn't cry the way she did all the time, for no reason at all. No one would make me work her long hours, on the dusty playgrounds with her charges, or teaching night school at White Sands Missile Range, having to travel over San Augustine Pass alone late at night, or peddling the *Encyclopedia Britannica* door to door during the weekends, with never any time to rest. Nor would I marry early like my older flat-footed sister, having four children by her mid-twenties. As for my young sister, her fate was sealed by her arch-less boat-length feet; she could never amount to much.

Feet dominated my life. My sister and I were always attendant to my Mother's bad legs, sore feet. As the older daughter at home, I was the one selected to pop my Mother's Morton's toes. She was always so grateful, saying, "Oh baby, thank you, you don't know, it helps so much."

Secretly, I didn't mind pulling and popping my Mother's toes in place, but I would never let on. I pretended it annoyed me and would make silly gestures as if to suggest her feet smelled. In actuality, popping her toes was a privilege accorded to me by my Mother. It was a vote of confidence and trust for the arch-worthy. These massages and toe pulls gave her tired, teacher's legs needed relief. She stood for hours every day and never sat down. She was always on the go and barely gave herself time to rest. She wore a girdle for countless years and at night she removed it warily, like taking off protective armor. And yet she often remarked that she didn't know what she would do without it.

Among various caregivers/ayudantes who took care of us was Belsora, a homely, plain-faced woman who tended happily to my Mother's feet. Belsora was from my Mother's hometown, El Polvo, Texas, and her features were as dry as the place of her birth. But a kinder, gentler woman was not to be found. When Belsora came into our lives, my Mother finally found someone who could tend to her the way my sister and I couldn't. Belsora didn't mind pulling my Mother's toes or massaging her feet, at all times of the day or night, with Vicks VapoRub. Mother got cramps in the middle of the night that made her call out in pain, waking up the entire house. "Ay, ay, los calamabres, ¡ay! Belsora, ¡ven! Come here! Hit my legs, hit them, I have cramps. Hit them! Harder!"

With bad legs come adjustments. Mother's shoe size grew through the years. I think she started off her adult life as a size eight, later moving to a nine, then a ten, on to an eleven and eventually a twelve. Because of her bad feet and dark-blue vein-covered legs, she had to change her shoes two and three times a day. When she found a shoe she liked, a shoe that was comfortable and fit her well, she would buy two and three pairs in different colors. Her closet was full of the same shoes. Shoes for a big, flat-footed, large-chested woman whose every step caused pain.

And yet, for all her discomfort, my Mother loved feet. Especially other people's feet. She loved to see a man or woman with pretty or handsome feet. She admired a good foot and was never shy about saying so.

In her later years, Mother talked about her feet wistfully, wondering how much longer she would be able to get around. She stood up unsteadily, finding her "land legs," as she said, as she lifted her heavy, earth-bound feet and struggled to move around without limping. Later, she condescended to use a cane. Elegant as ever, majestic with her carved wooden bordón, a family heirloom, she would take a rest, pause gratefully, and gently sigh:

"Thank you, God, for my feet, whatever they're like. They go all the way to the ground, and that's all that matters. Now you, you're still young, Denise. You have good feet, and an arch. You and your Father. You're the lucky ones."

Ensalada/Salad

Salad Memories

My Mother wasn't a salad person. I don't recall ever eating many salads at our house. I had to call my sister Margo to ask if we ever ate salad. She seemed certain about seeing an occasional one. The only lettuce Mother ever used was iceberg. I never knew anything about fancy lettuces: no radicchio, frisée, endive or baby greens. I never ate butter lettuce until I was thirty years old. Artichokes? They came from another planet.

Mother would take a chunk of iceberg, cut it with a knife, something you are not supposed to do—or rather, gourmets have told us not to do—and put it in a bowl. She'd cut up a few tomatoes and throw those in. We never had fancy salad dressings. I think we used either mayonnaise or Hellmann's sandwich spread.

Our lettuce was local. It was grown in the Mesilla Valley and it was always inexpensive. What my Mother knew best, and what she loved all her life, was known food, like the melons from her home state, grown in the hottest place in Texas—and for that matter all the U.S.—by my Tío Manuel Franco. Texas water, too, was unparalleled; it was the best water in the world, what she called "Good Texas Water."

I've chopped lettuce and shredded it to smithereens while more than one person has looked askance at my lettuce-cutting methods. The husband of a friend looked at me like I was crazy when I cut up an onion in front of him. I never realized I could offend anyone by dicing an onion. I have also been yelled at by a persnickety relative for "cutting," not "tearing," lettuce. What did I know about lettuce or the way it needed to be de-leafed, not cut? I attribute my lack of salad eating today to the days of no salads. I realize we never had a sharp knife in the house, let alone a salad knife. We sharpened what knives we had, and they were a sad-looking bunch, on the edge of the cement step near the laundry room that led to the Blue Room.

In high school and college, I was the designated occasional chef, and often I made my two specialties: meat loaf chock-full of sliced vegetables or pot roast. The pot roast was cooked in an electric skillet that was a Christmas gift from my Father. I'd crowd the pan of either the meat loaf or pot roast with potatoes, carrots, onions and zucchini. They would tenderize as the meat cooked. I always seared my meat first and then slow-cooked it. I'm not bragging, but I was good at these two dishes. Comida Mexicana was my Mother's specialty, and I was merely her sous-chef.

As a result of my limited cooking experience, I knew little about international food. What I knew best was my Mother's food, the food she loved all her life, and it was from her I learned to cook it. Las Cruces only had two kinds of restaurants then: Mexican and hamburgers. Asian food, Italian food, any other kind of food? Forget it!

We were a family who ate fast most of the time, and on special occasions—and there were many—we always ate tacos.

When Tacos Are Tacos

In general terms, and the phrase is very subjective, tacos are just that, tacos. But a taco from a kit or popular taquería may be very different if you live in southern or northern New Mexico, New York or Paris, France. Most of the best tacos are to be found at home, unless of course you and your family never learned to make tacos.

Making a good taco is like being a good dancer. You have to practice with your mother, brother, sister or friends to learn how to dance. Most people do not become seasoned taco-istas or dancers without some practice. There are exceptions, of course, like my husband, who never learned to dance with either mother, father, brother or friend. What he did learn was how to cook. Of French and Russian ancestry, he knew the preparation of a good meal was critical to family life. Daniel has become a good taquero, and what he is known for is his salsa. It's really good.

Daniel usually helps me roll tacos, and from time to time I will find the cara of the tortilla on the outside. When I am in a hurry I sometimes am guilty of the same indiscretion, and always, I think of my Mother, standing over me—the woman could hover and hence my nickname for her—The Eagle—as she checked out the symmetry and grace of my tacos as they lay in baking sheets ready to go into a hot oven.

Making tacos is a graceful dance. And eating a good taco is a joy. This Thanksgiving I prepared both turkey and tacos. The tacos, by far, were our most satisfying meal. You can get tired of turkey but never of a good taco.

Así es. And so it is.

Salsa Daniel

About 1 pound fresh tomatoes or 1 pound canned, peeled whole tomatoes

About a half dozen Big Jim chiles, peeled and roasted. Big Jim is a variety of chile that is tasty and fleshy. You can substitute any other chile that is available, the fresher the better.

1 or 2 cloves garlic

About a handful of cilantro

Salt to taste

Dice the tomatoes to salsa consistency.

Chop the peeled roasted green chiles. You can decide if you want mild, medium, hot or hazardous.

Finely chop the garlic and add to the mixture.

Chop the cilantro.

Add salt.

Mix all ingredients together.

Enjoy!

Salsa Daniel is a very subjective, personal recipe. Daniel is not a rigid person about chile or cooking, so you have to decide about how hot you want your chile to be and what the consistency of the salsa should be. If you have any questions, ask him.

Daniel's approach to life is similar to the Dalai Lama's: "Approach love and cooking with insouciant abandon."

The Word Taco

The word taco in the *Random House Word Menu* is defined as "a Mexican dish of fried tortilla that is folded and filled with a mixture of meat, cheese and salad."

The word taco is not understood by all, and it can mean different things in different places. A friend, Olin Calk, says that in Mississippi tacos are called "bend-ups."

We never ate folded tacos at our house; they were always rolled. I did eat folded tacos elsewhere, and while I consider them tacos, they aren't *my* tacos.

The word taco, then, means different things to different people. Another friend, Jorge Robles, born in México, has informed me of the many uses of the word taco. One could write a whole book about "taco-isms." And I think Jorge should and will. As a matter of fact, we need to have a Part II of *A Taco Testimony*, which will include taco stories from the readers of this book. No doubt Jorge will be involved, as he knows a taco from a taco.

The word taco has many popular and sexual connections. On the female side, there are many words for a sanitary napkin in Spanish, including the most popular, toalla sanitaria. But they are also referred to as "tacos" or "tamales."

On the male side, a taco or flauta, with any added number of colorful adjectives or used singularly, is a penis. It can also be used to describe the fold in a woman's body that envelops a "taco."

Given my Mother's proper upbringing and spirituality, my sister and I were not privy to the popular vernacular terms for tacos. Mother never scared us with stories of La Llorona, the weeping woman by the river who drowned her children, or of the boogeyman, the fearful cucuy. We never heard of a chupacabra. A cabra, sí, but a chupacabra, a blood-sucking monster, no.

A taco sí, but that kind of taco, no. All words and their meanings came to us in a pure undiluted proper form, as seen through the eyes and heart of my very circumspect and culturally diligent Mother. "Please, Denise!" I can hear my Mother's voice admonishing me. "Ya, ¡por favor! A taco is just that, a taco!"

Tacos Throughout

For many years my Father did and then didn't live with us, and then he came to visit often and then not at all. In the early years of my parents' divorce, Daddy would stay with us without any sense of discomfort or remorse. He probably slept with my Mother throughout all this time; they weren't divorced, so why not? I remember him sheepishly slipping out of my Mother's bedroom even into their later years.

If my Father was visiting, he would stay a very short time. His visits coincided with the holidays or his birthday, which to him and to us was the biggest holiday of all.

Later on, he stayed with his sister Elsie, or sometimes with his brother Lalo. He mostly stayed with Uncle Lalo and Aunt Mela when he was married to Ruth, his Mormon wife and drinking partner. Sometimes he stayed in a motel on Picacho Street near a former drinking hole. When he stayed with us he stayed in the den, his former study room at the back of the house.

The den later became my Mother's junk room, but Daddy never cared. He once nailed a set of curtains to the wall of his duplex in Albuquerque. What did he care about décor? It didn't matter that you couldn't open the curtains and that they were forever closed; they were "up" and that was all that mattered. He was a notoriously bad housekeeper, so it didn't concern him that he was resting in a room full of yard tools, piles of old yellowed newspaper and my Mother's colorful sewing scraps. The room was at the back of the house and it had its own private entrance, something he, no doubt, enjoyed.

It was the middle time that was the most difficult for us all. This was when my Father was married to a woman who wasn't my Mother. Ruth was a fiery redhead with a small, tight body, and she was my Father's drinking equal. They were a nasty team. And yet, I honestly believe that they loved each other.

It's hard to ascertain the depth of my Father's devotion or love for any human being, especially a woman. He was bound—heart and soul—to the drink. Anyone or anything, almost anything, came second. His work came first, but barely. He squeaked by and for many years was able to maintain his two mistresses: drink and work. It was only later that he began to unravel. There were those wild nights and feverish binges in the early days, but they blew in and out like the wind. Alas, when you live in the desert Southwest, the wind always catches up with you. It was only later that my Father's world was constantly grey, the pale grey of bad weather, cloud-filled skies, a sad, rambling disorder of night and day, neglect and compensation, punctuated by Blessed Mother Sleep or Merciful Drink.

So—what does this history have to do with tacos?

It's always back to the tacos. Tacos are my life and my story. They are my hope. They are my salvation, and I don't say that lightly. They are my history. My culture. They are who I am. They are my roots and my Becoming. My pride and my healing.

It's so good to be Mexican.

Little man:
Your eyes are browned earth
Your age the sun
Your hands
Stained leather
Wood
Your sighs
Vaporous vaults of sorrow

You are my dying grandfather
Walking across town
With a sack of popsicles
For us
My Father telling me this
His teeth bitten down and dark

He had teeth like pearls
My Mother said
He had this smile you would not believe
She looked away
Smiled then
Smiled them

The Night of the Tacos

You shouldn't be angry when you cook tacos. It's best to cook Mexican food in a neutral mood or state of being. Impatience or irritation has never helped tacos along. Making tacos can be messy, so you want to avoid being imbalanced when you work with hot grease. Nor should you be around anyone who is angry. One misstep and either of you could be marked for life. A slip of any kind and there goes what could have been a wonderful and memorable meal. High emotion can destroy more than relationships.

When cooking tacos you should never be flustered or hostile either, although I have to say I have made tacos in all these states, as well as when I was sad, lost and depressed. Tacos have brought me back from the brink, and I mean that literally.

When I was in graduate school I had a very hard time of it. I never ate well and suffered from some sort of eating disorder, probably lack of proper nourishment that, fed by depression, was exacerbated by the fact I lacked a basic belief in myself and suffered from insecurity and nerves. I rarely ate breakfast, and when I got to the theatre where I worked in what I considered slavery in the costume shop, I would drink a cup of instant hot chocolate. This held me until lunch, when I might have another cup of hot chocolate. I don't remember eating much then. Maybe I ate something at a cast party or a sponsor's reception at the theatre school I was attending. I might have a sandwich or some soup when I got home in the evenings. My lack of appetite was a symptom of my deeper and greater unhappiness.

I was on a tight scholarship that afforded little in the way of anything extra. Occasionally my Mother would send me a little money, as well as a token dollar bill in the cards and letters she sent me. This tender and reassuring act meant so much to me.

I remember I didn't eat ice cream for months on end; I just couldn't afford any luxury foods of any type. Back then, I had never tasted mellorine and once bought a pint to try it out. That was about all I could afford. The chalky-tasting orange-flavored mellorine was a weak substitute for real ice cream, and I sobbed to myself with irritation for being so poor.

During that time, I was often very unhappy, although in retrospect, I had so much: a scholarship to graduate school, a life's calling to be in theatre and a handsome, tall, blond boyfriend from Yonkers, New York, who was a leather artist. What else could I wish for? Few other women in the theatre department had a boyfriend, and I had snagged mine right out of the graduate school chute. Or rather, he had snagged me. Later he told me it was the sky-blue polyester sailor pantsuit with matching top I was wearing when he first saw me that had endeared me to him. Despite no lack of romance with one of the school's hunks, I was terribly sad all the time. I was a low woman, very low on an ethnic and hierarchical totem pole that didn't include young Chicana women like myself who were outspoken and never satisfied with the unspoken, unbroken overriding Anglo status quo. And on top of everything, I was a rebellious mocosa, a snot-nosed snit who believed herself better than anyone else. But I wasn't, of course. I was just an artistic neophyte with a little more pleito in her than anyone wanted to see or cared to admit. The theatre director once greeted me with the phrase, "Here's my enemy." I didn't understand what he was saying and yet I did. I knew I would just have to endure the slings and arrows of being a rebel child among the chosen few if I wanted to get my degree. The old bowling metaphors that I still use today came out of this time period: forward glide, good follow-through, ball in the right place, you know where it goes, don't deviate and—strike! You did it! I've often seen my degrees as bowling trophies.

During that time I was homesick and heartsick all the time. But I knew I had to stick graduate school out. I couldn't go home, even though I wanted to.

This was one of my Cheez Whiz periods. There have been others, but this was the most sustained. I largely subsisted on marijuana and leftover theatre cast party food, which included a lot of potato chips and all sorts of sour-cream-based dips with the occasional vegetable side, which might consist of carrots, cucumbers, cauliflower or broccoli diced every which way and set in the middle of a large revolving lazy Susan. The three years I was in graduate school were years of bad eating, no eating. I was a mess.

One particularly bad night I felt myself unraveling. I was in trouble and knew it. I couldn't keep up with my studies, all I wanted to do was sleep, and on top of everything else, I was avoiding going to class. In those days, most everyone smoked marijuana all the time. The crowd I hung around with had more than enough to go around. We spent our days and nights away from school and rehearsals hanging out at someone's house watching television, eating and laughing ourselves silly.

The only other time I had smoked marijuana was in college at my wild and wonderful friend Jerry's house during a study session for a Spanish exam. His parents were in the living room and unbeknownst to them, we were toking up in the den over the past imperfect. My Mother had left me off and later picked me up when I was in the middle of an incredible virgin high. I remember the car appeared very small as all the car doors disappeared. I floated home in an ether dream and noticed the street curbs were as tall as cathedrals. I barely made it to my bedroom, which was at the back of the house through an incredibly long hallway.

But that was nothing compared to my new life as a pseudo hip graduate student with delusions of grandeur and an avocation for the surreal. Gradually I moved on to other drugs. Once while smoking hash I transformed into my belt. I knew belt-dom, and I don't say that lightly. It was probably during this time that I developed my uncanny sense of smell as a snuff jar was passed around. I walked up to an old tapestry and discerned the strata of its years, and it was more than I could bear. I am thankful I never got close to the Lady of the Unicorn tapestries in France.

I had started to get dizzy spells. I would become terrified when I entered new places. Sometimes I couldn't eat. And once, while in an elevator headed to the twenty-something-th floor of a cast party in a fancy hotel, I noticed my hands had turned blue.

This state of affairs reached its culmination on this one terrible night. I was seriously distressed and tried to communicate this to my boyfriend, who shrugged it off. I don't think he knew how bad off I was.

What saved me was the fact that I had to make tacos. I can't remember why I had to make tacos but I did. I had bought the meat, the tortillas, everything I needed. My boyfriend stayed with me through the taco-making nightmare. I would freak out, try to lie down, and then remember that I had to finish the tacos. These up and down movements punctuated what seemed an interminable stretch of time. I knew that if I did lie down and give in to It, whatever the It was that was going on, a breakdown of sorts, I knew that then I would have trouble coming back. There was no one to call. I could have called my Mother, she was counselor for many years on a Christian hot line for troubled people, but I preferred not to. My family lived over a thousand miles away, and I didn't want to upset her with a call telling her I was cracking up. My boyfriend didn't really understand what was going on, or maybe he did, but he didn't want to admit it. Despite all this, he stayed with me, and for that I am grateful. To say I was frantic is an understatement. As I mashed the taco meat and added my comino, I seriously doubted I'd see the tacos through. But I did. I finished cooking the taco meat, then rolled the tacos, and only then, having spent my illness on the taco making, only then did I go to bed.

Tacos can save your life. They did mine that night.

I realize now that I was very ill. The reasons are many, more than I can ever explain, but a great deal of my trouble then had to do with a bad diet, overwhelming sadness, a loss of identity, and a disembodiment that I attribute to my incredible lack of confidence in myself. My soul had flown away and I hadn't realized it. I had come from a college where I was one of the top students, an actress who got many acting roles, who was supported by community and family, and now I was in a place where I found myself alone and insecure—rootless, really—save for the tacos that represented the known and the loved. Those midnight tacos were my desperate connection, my umbilical cord to who I was and would always be.

Drugs can cause you to lose yourself, and so can abject loneliness and lack of self-worth. After I started taking drugs, I became addicted to the wanting to belong to those who belonged. To what I am not sure. And I did belong, for a while, to a little hip clique that took drugs and were proud of it. When we saw each other we greeted each other knowing we were The Ones: the sophisticated, worldly ones, the seers, the artists, the chosen ones. But it was all pretension, delusion and illusion. I never felt secure in those days and drugs only made things worse. I felt worthless and ugly. Drugs and/or graduate school can both do that to you.

I don't think I've known such abject worthlessness since then.

I knew after a while, early on, that I couldn't support a drug habit, and that it couldn't even be an occasional vice. I grew more frightened than euphoric and saw doors opening up when doors weren't there. Three doors always surrounded me. Each room I found myself in had three doors, and in my frazzled state of mind, I began to find a terrible significance in the three doors that seemed to follow me everywhere. I found myself absent, as if I had stepped out of one of those three doors and had gone missing. It was a sad, shabby time and I'm not proud of it.

And yet, I held on, one of only three people in my class to get a graduate degree after three years. I don't know how I did it—yes—I do: the forward glide, the follow-through, knowing where to place the ball. I attribute my persistence, my undying, underlying faith in the good for saving me and turning round my life that night I made the tacos.

When I was deep in my misery and in need of help, the slow, ritualistic, repetitive and blessed familiarity of tacos, of where I'd come from, of my rootedness, took hold and helped me back from darkness. Angels stood with me by the stove, their invisible hands on mine, and their breath, that small almost imperceptible breeze of hope, lingered in that gloomy humid night in my sad little apartment and bound me to my destiny. I would finish making the tacos! I would get my master's degree! I would leave my lonely life behind! I would come home! I would become a writer and I would remember!

I was a lucky one. I've seen many friends and some family members lose their way and sometimes their lives with drugs. I was one of the lucky ones. I walked through one of those doors and never looked back. And when I think of that large round Taco Table in our dining room and those who sat there with me who left us too early because of one drug or another, I know that it wasn't my fate to continue that path, and for that, I am grateful.

And when I lose my way, and I still do, for there are always days of sadness and despair, with little hope in sight, in the constant undertow of this roiling sea of life, I remember that night of the tacos. I remember how I turned back to the self that knew what she was doing and how to do it. My faith was and is a thing familiar, as familiar and sacred as a corn tortilla on a hot comal.

There have been other times when tacos and the love of family have saved my life. My Mother once saw me through a bad pneumonia. I was living away from home but returned home very ill for her to take care of me. She let me sleep in her room and nursed me back to health. My illness was grave, but I couldn't talk to anyone about it. I even received the last rites, the Catholic sacrament given to those who are mortally ill. I am not sure I was that sick, but I have to say I was helped immensely by the grace of that blessing. I could feel the small flame of hope flicker in my heart, and I knew I would get better. Mother and I never talked about it much. I was too sick to want to talk, even if I could. Mother let me find my way back to health. Her food helped me and surely jump-started the healing.

As anyone knows, tacos can cure you if you have a cruda, a hangover of any kind. They can soften your sadness, ease the pain and set the brokenness in you back on the bed where it can rest awhile and then go to sleep like an overheated, petulant child, a child that doesn't know how deeply it is hurting itself. Amen, amen I say. Amen.

La Macha Grande

Macho: masculine, vigorous, robust, male. (Mexican dictionary, 1967)
Macho: overtly assertive, virile, domineering. (English dictionary, 1968)
Macho: me, woman/man, navigating two cultures, two worldviews, two antiquated
    dictionaries from the twentieth century. (Denise Chávez, 2006)

I never knew the meaning of the word macho until the late sixties. I wasn't an activist; I was a drama major. While I deplored the war in Vietnam, I was still trying to figure out how to keep my wiglet looking good, the tight curls in place, not too lacquered down, not too obviously not real. My false eyelashes occasionally buckled at the edges, and once I made the mistake of falling asleep with them on. My eyes were nearly permanently stuck together in the morning.

In those days everyone wore the same buff-colored, grainy-textured pantyhose that pouched out horribly at the knees. I wore a girdle to hold them in place in those days before pantyhose were perfected. No Queen-Size-Ivory-Nude-to-the-Waist-Control-Tops. In those days nothing ever fit me well. The Kotex were never secure, a floppy rubber belt supposedly holding them in place. Too often I had to reach up the middle of my back and yank that defiant cotton pad down, down!

In those days macho was my Mother. To Mother, macho *was not* my Father. Macho was *her* father, Eusebio Rede, a coal miner from Redford, Texas. Macho to

Eusebio was *his* father, Nabor Rede, a man who had to tell his wife, on noticing that the Apaches were coming down the cerro toward him with rifles drawn, to tie her shawl around their son, "Fájate bien el rebozo, porque vamos a correr." She tied her shawl around her son, Eusebio, and run they did, down the mountain to freedom, home. Nabor had laid his rifle across his waist, knowing that if he didn't reach the bottom of the hill he would have to kill his wife and child, he so wanted to spare them whatever pain they might have to endure. Now *that* was macho.

It's sad for me to think that nativo killed nativo in those days, but it was so.

One has to wonder if life has changed so much.

Today macho is a mad dog named Cujo, a character out of a Stephen King novel, running after you, flinging his raging, senseless animal body at you as you try to escape, quick to the car, where you lock the windows, let out a sigh of relief, and then realize the creature is jumping toward you outside the insecure safety of the glass, his slobber running down the sides of the car, just when you thought you were safe. You know you'll only be able to stay in the car so long, you'll need to eat, go to the bathroom, get away, and when you try, there he'll be, a rabid creation of what you imagine is fictionalized life, and dammit, you once loved dogs!

Macho definitely wasn't me, in my late twenties, living with a man who just had to go see his old girlfriend in California. The day he left by bus I went next door to pay our rent to our landlady, her crazy Doberman coming out of nowhere and punching me with strong front legs, taking the breath out of me as the landlady came out to see what was happening. What was happening? I was paying the rent for someone who didn't love me! And not only that, I had to endure the chisme about him, the mitote and gossip I couldn't hear about until it was nearly too late.

You should be married. Translation = You are living in sin, and not only that, it's unlikely he'll marry you anyway.

You should wear a bra. Translation = You have the breasts of a married woman. Unmarried women have small nipples, no dark areolas. It's obvious you've spent yourself on the altar of lust with this mixed-breed without pedigree.

Becoming macho for me meant having to endure interminable susurros/ whispers from relatives: cousins, so-called friends, male and female. Some of them were almost truth. And always there was that push, like that mad Doberman, your own Cujo nightmare, taking the silent breath out of you, except you couldn't show anyone that you were in pain, or that what people said hurt.

When I was young and vulnerable there were too many critical comments about my face, my body and my attempt to find lifelong work that sustained the heart. If it wasn't a leering cousin making lewd remarks about my chichis or telling me he saw me sleeping, my nightgown pulled up high to my thighs, it was my tío or tía laughing at my fly-by-night jobs, my so-called "career."

The push of macho is still real. The myth is that it is a romantic ideal, a bad metaphor and a cliché. The sadness is that both men and women are still playing out this cliché and think it is their birthright. A salivating, hyperventilating dog, crazed with the scent of blood. I pulled the Kotex down, tried to hang on, like all my bleeding sisters, to the sanctity of womanhood, and to the men who knew what real strength meant.

My Mother's old macho refrain comes to mind: Know your priorities. Y m'ijita, por el amor de Dios, always have your own money. I touch the long remembered dime in my little beaded sixties handbag. I am transported to those days when a dime was all you needed to call home. At the other end of the line was your Mother, La Macha Grande, who waited for you with bated breath, not wanting you to hurt the way she did.

Plato Fuerte/Main Course

In Praise of Tacos

My Mother died much too early, at age 73, of liver cancer. Doctor Angel told us she had once contracted hepatitis and had probably never taken care of herself. Probably she'd lived with the illness all her life. I don't think she knew she had it.

My Father returned to live two houses down from my Mother the year before her death. In my mind and heart, I know his return hastened her death. I can't help feeling that if he hadn't moved back, she might have lived longer. But this is only conjecture.

She came to visit me the winter before she died, in Santa Fe where I was living. I found her crying in my bedroom, but I wasn't astute enough to realize the bloody Kleenex in the bathroom wastebasket signaled her decline.

First she developed a cancer on her lip and had it removed. But she rapidly lost weight. During this time she asked me to write something for the dedication of Immaculate Heart of Mary Cathedral in Las Cruces and the investiture of Bishop Ramírez. I wrote two short plays: *La Morenita,* about Our Lady of Guadalupe, and a piece called *Francis!* about the life of St. Francis. This was her last major request of me, although I didn't know it at the time, and I was happy to comply.

In the months of March and April just prior to Mother's death, my sister Margo and I toured in a play called *Hecho en México,* a mariachi musical about undocumented women workers, a play I had written with the actress Nita Luna. When my Mother was dying in the hospital those last inexorable two weeks, we had to tear ourselves away to perform the play around the state. We did bring my Mother home one weekend, and the cast cleared out the living room and we performed for an audience of two, my Mother and older sister. That night we took Mother to her bedroom to rest and the cast brought out food. We had a feast around the Taco Table as my Mother was dying in her blue bedroom. Mother was in a coma the last week or so and was unable to talk. But the night before she died, she rallied, came out of her coma, and was able to talk to my sister and me. Both of us had been sleeping outside her room on cots in the hallway.

Mother looked up at me and told me with great love, "Denise, you have such pretty eyes." I have always been grateful to her for coming back to us that night to say goodbye and for that gift of blessing she bestowed upon me as she lay in her deathbed, her words of pain etched in my heart: "What an ordeal."

Death was a terrible tribulation for her, as she lay in bed with a huge, bloated stomach, unable to talk, unable to move. And yet, she returned briefly, magically, to us that last night, and for that mercy there are no words. And the further irony was the fact she had cirrhosis of the liver. She, who never drank, she who couldn't stand drunks and had to live with one all her life, she had died of what was perceived as a disease of alcoholics. The irony of her illness has never failed to impress me.

Maybe she'd drunk just a little, a drink that she didn't know was a drink, like the Toritos we drank together in México City, those tasty fruit and alcohol concoctions that sneak up on you and make you silly and giggly; or a sip of her brother Beto's homemade vino tinto or maybe an occasional glass of overly sweet Mogen David wine in the presence of her mother's sister, her Tía Manina, a hunchbacked little woman who came to live with us one summer. My sister Margo had been given a prescription of sweet wine for her appetite. She had mononucleosis and wasn't eating. Margo hated the wine that was her tonic, and we all knew that Manina raided the refrigerator surreptitiously and drank my sister's wine supply whenever she could. She was an old woman, in her late eighties, and who was there to stop her?

———•◦•◦•———

Mother died April 26, 1983. I resented that I never had any time alone with her those last weeks before she died. So many people surrounded her in her hospital room. She was deeply loved and no one ever wanted to leave her side. There were interminable prayer meetings, songfests, rosaries, blessings, tears, noise, noise, noise. Too many comings and goings, the buzz and flurry were endless. There was no quiet time for her or for me. I wanted everyone to disappear so I could hold her hand, stroke her face and tell her how much I loved her. Too many things I had to say. Things left unsaid. And when she died in the afternoon, surrounded by balloons one of her friends had bought for her, it was I who carried them out into the sunlight, my heart burdened by trapped words that floated thickly through the anguished air.

And later, when I was alone in her house, I locked all the doors, and for hours I cried out and talked to her, as I wept hard tears of dismay, immeasurable grief and incredible sadness, and told her, in a loud and audible voice, through my sobs of despair, the many things I hadn't been able to tell her in the crowded, people-weary hospital room, that unforgettable death room, where my dying mother sought her peace, as she rolled out to the great sea, her breath a wave that lingered, came in, lingered, came in and eventually swept away, and left me, stunned and devastated, with my burden of living.

What followed were tacos. Hundreds came our way, from family, friends, even from people I didn't know. We didn't cook for a week. Our family was surrounded by food, engulfed by food, and we fed multitudes.

Little by little, day after day, I came back from the brink of immense sadness to enjoy life and food again, but that took years. I wasn't able to find my moorings until several years after my Mother's death. Again, I had an eating disorder. I simply could not eat because I was so sad. It was like anorexia but worse. I wasn't throwing up, and I did lose a lot of weight, but it wasn't for beauty or my own personal sake. I was just really sad.

Life lost its luster and joy. And only over time, little by little, as I began to reflect on the blessings of my life and engage once again in joyful action, I began to start eating again. My hunger for living returned as I started to say grace before each meal. I forgot my wounded self-despair and learned to live again. This wasn't before I had done much soul-searching. This was after countless prayer sessions, much therapy and several spiritual retreats, one of them at Glorieta, New Mexico, that changed my life.

It wasn't until I went on the retreat that I realized I was angry with my Father for my Mother's death. He didn't actually kill her; it was worry over him that did. Also, my Mother was immensely tired. Her body was failing her and she knew it. What we, her family, didn't realize was how very fragile and vulnerable she was. Life with and without my Father had worn her out. I could analyze the reasons for my Mother's obsession with him, but everything comes up short. She was agotada/exhausted and ready to move on. She didn't want to live a long life. She had trouble walking and dreaded the day she wouldn't be able to walk. She was simply ready to die, although she feared it. And despite that fear, her faith sustained her and gave her immeasurable peace that supported her in that last torturous movement toward Death.

A five-day healing retreat at Glorieta Conference Center with a set of twin priests, the Lynn brothers, was a last-ditch effort on my part to find my way back from sadness. We were asked to find someone who reminded us of the person we most needed to forgive. I searched around for someone who looked like my Father. No one reminded me of him. Ah, yes … there was one bedraggled-looking older man who hung around the back of the church during all the sessions, trying to escape. We were two of a kind, rebels with a cause, procrastinators by will, who only by chance found ourselves at the back of the church trying as hard as we could to find our way out the door, some kind of salvation. The man was disheveled, seedy-looking, and seemed so out of place. He was perfect! I decided that he was the person whose feet I would wash.

I hardly slept that first night; I tossed and turned in a deep sweat. My roommate, a lovely older woman, told me that what I was experiencing was normal, to be expected, given the great upheaval I had been through. The following day I approached the old man, the foot-washing assignate, and asked if I could wash his feet. He told me that it was not possible, that he had a fungus on his feet. I was shocked! It was too perfect! My Father had a fungus on his feet as well. And so I would be washing the man's hands instead of his feet.

Several days passed as I attended the sessions in a confusion of pain and deep reflection. I won't say it was a good time, but it was a necessary time. Finally, on the last day everyone lined up to wash the feet of the person who represented the person they needed to forgive. It was quite a lineup. I stood next to the unkempt viejito and took his gnarled, calloused hands in my own.

Some time afterwards, I learned with some horror he was a priest. ¡Ay! And not only that, the man was an alcoholic as well. ¡Ay! When I washed his hands a great heaviness lifted from me and I felt better. ¡Ay, ay, ay!

Other things happened during that time, things that brought me back to life, miraculous things. I made new friends and returned home a different person. After two years of mourning my Mother's death, there was a marked change in my life direction. I got married, although I had never wanted to ever marry. Another thing that happened was that I was able to begin to love my Father again and, in turn, myself. On reflection, it was never my Father I was angry with; it was myself—for being so insensitive and unaware of my Mother's distress and impending death. I had seen the bloody Kleenex in her wastebasket. I had heard her crying, seen her sadness, was aware she was altered, ill. What did I think was going on?

I have never forgotten those days in Glorieta, learning to eat and to forgive. After that I was able to move on with life. It was time. Tacos awaited.

I gradually accepted my Mother's death, her "ordeal" as she called it, her terrible and arduous passage, as well as the great responsibility that awaited me as my Father's caregiver for fifteen years.

Those years have indelibly marked me, as have the memories of meals at the round Taco Table in my Father's dining room. His home was two houses down from mine. I never knew where I should be, in what house, his or mine. When I was at his house, I felt I should be at mine. And when I was at mine, I felt I should be at his. I would lose things and remember they were at the Other House. Where was the bread? Oh, it's over *there*. I thought it was *here*. Over there, over there. For fifteen years I lived between houses and between Taco Tables. And throughout all those years so many people cared for Mr. C., including the woman who was to become my best friend, Constance Marie Gale, who was with us for ten years. Hundreds of helpers came and went. My Father was well taken care of, and although it was a struggle to keep his household going, we survived. Once again, I experienced tacos at a large, round table, albeit in another house, with a unique vecino, my Father, Mr. E. E. C.

The Old Rascal

As a teenager, and most particularly as a rebellious college student, I wanted to break every strand linking me to family and culture. Maybe not so much culture as family. Hell, I just wanted to leave home!

I wanted to go far away, and I tried. My first attempt was to apply to Loretto High School in El Paso. A highly respected Catholic girls' school, it taught the daughters of the elite of both El Paso and Juárez, as well as anyone else who was accepted and could pay the tuition. Mother allowed me to take the entrance exam, although I knew we didn't have the money for me to attend. I appreciated her gesture of goodwill.

The morning of the exam I couldn't eat and felt sick to my stomach. The early-morning drive to El Paso was interminable, as it sometimes can be. I felt very cold and alone as I sat in the alien classroom taking the exam. I remembered my Mother's advice: pray that you are only asked the questions you know.

The only thing that warmed me up was a stop at our favorite neighborhood restaurant in El Paso, La Paloma. In my mind, I have an eternal reverence for this humble but wonderful joint. It's been closed for a long time, and yet the memory of sitting in the warm plastic booths is comforting. We were regulars. La Paloma's tacos and burritos were legendary and each plate was large and tasty. As ever, Mother was on a limited budget. But this didn't stop us from enjoying a lunch or dinner at La Paloma on Delta Street just off Paisano. The restaurant was close to my Tío Mundo and Tía Esperanza's house as well as my cousin Yvonne's. If we weren't in a hurry and spent the weekend in El Paso, usually when my Tía Chita would come to visit from El Polvo, we'd take a room at the McCoy Hotel, right off the Plaza de Lagartos, where once old and crusty alligators held court in a small, low cement pond smack-dab in the middle of busy downtown El Paso.

There was something perverse and wonderful about the pond. It was a gathering place for everyone that came through El Paso on the way to Juárez, just across the Stanton Street Bridge. Or it was a landmark that signified that you'd made it once more across to Los Estados Unidos, where a better life awaited—cleaning houses or toilets, doing someone's laundry or working at any number of lower-paying jobs that still paid higher than in México.

During Christmastime the plaza was full of Christmas lights that hung from every tree and light post. To one side was a giant tree with enormous multi-colored bulbs, and around the plaza were placed various tableaux: a manger scene with Mary, Joseph and the Baby Jesus; another with Santa Claus and his industrious elves. The plaza was only an illusionary winter wonderland, because sometimes on Christmas Day the temperature might be in the low 70s. We grew up with fake snow, powdered dreams and the inert, lethargic lagartos in the plaza, slow-moving, barely breathing. Like the snow, they too represented a bizarre dream from another world, not our own.

We stayed at the McCoy Hotel, which was located next to the Plaza movie theatre, an elegant movie house that showed the latest, most popular movies in English. Plush red seats, a red carpet and a painted mural on either side of the stage marked it clearly as the most luxurious theatre in the area.

Just down the street was El Teatro Colón, the Mexican movie house that showed popular movies in Spanish featuring Mexican film stars Pedro Infante, Dolores Del Río, Pedro Armendáriz and María Félix. The movie house was built on the site of a former Chinese cemetery, in what is our region's Asian town, over the graves of Chinese immigrants who came to the border area after the Civil War to work on the railroads. In my research on El Colón for my novel *Loving Pedro Infante*, the owner, John "Juan" Salom, who is of Lebanese and Mexican descent, told me that when El Colón closed in 1979, they turned the front part of the lobby into a small restaurant named Super Torta. The workers who were digging into the foundation found the body of what they believed to be a small child. Instead, it turned out to be the body of a tiny Chinese woman.

Across the street from El Colón, popular as the theatre of the people, was the Alcazar Theatre, known as "El Calcetín," named for its supposed smell of dirty socks. The movie house catered to soldiers from Fort Bliss and to blacks.

I never went to El Calcetín and I only later learned of its dubious fame. The special and individual nature of each of the three theatres appealed to different classes of people. But that was something that I, as a child, couldn't articulate but could only wonder about. Children are aware of discrimination, racism and class structure, and what I learned about all these things came from my wandering around El Paso, Texas, and my Mother's hometown in Far West Texas. The more subtle, imperceptible discrimination of my hometown of Las Cruces was so veiled and discreet it was rarely seen or discussed. As a result, the population was more deracinated than in the other places that were part of my life.

How odd! To be a Mexicano in Far West Texas meant you held on to and venerated your Mother Culture more, while to be a Mexicano in southern New Mexico, forty-two miles from the Mexican border at Ciudad Juárez, Chihuahua, meant for my Father's family, at least, that he and his clan moved away from their native roots, their language and the myriad beautiful components of their culture. I've often wondered how my Mother could retain her cultural history while my Father lost his. This inquiry has led me down the path of recognition that not everyone is a cultured person and that culture has nothing to do with whether one is rich or poor or born on one side of town or another.

My Mother's family was born in the dust of Texas, nothing in sight but cactus and the Chisos Mountains, and I consider them the most cultured people I have ever known. What is the reason? Literacy. Education. Appreciation for the written and spoken word. And a willingness to explore other diverse and distinct worlds.

My Mother moved effortlessly through a multiplicity of life experiences with all sorts of people, with a fluidity that is admirable. She sat comfortably in the kitchens of the most humble wooden shacks in any number of vecindades in Juárez or Ojinaga or México City or in the colonias of our own U.S.A., eating a warm tortilla with people who had very little. She enjoyed a good hot comida corriente chicharrón taco on El Paso Street near El Colón, at the taquería that had huge sides of pork skins hanging in the windows. And she enjoyed a plato especial in the best of Juárez' restaurants in her day, or in the large beautiful mansions on La Calle Diez y Seis de Septiembre, with other ladies in large hats and white gloves, her hermanas from the Pan American Round Table, as the clubs did their intercambios with their sister organizations.

Sometimes we'd drive by an opulent barricaded house with its adjacent guest houses, tiled pools and immense well-kept grounds, and Mother would say, "I've been inside that house."

Mother was a woman whose word was firm. I wish I could say I am as fiel, as steady. When she made a pronouncement, it was engraved in stone. The only times she ever vacillated had to do with my Father, and that was only early on in their divorced life. She eventually steeled herself against him as well, although she kept waiting for him to come home. And by God, he finally did.

Daddy had always been part of our taco lives. He showed up during the important and celebratory times: Valentine's Day, Fourth of July, Thanksgiving, Christmas and birthdays, most especially his. He would arrive in his pea-green Pontiac, which my Mother nicknamed "Jaws" for the movie popular at the time.

Jaws had been rear-ended, circumstances unknown, and the trunk was held down by an uncoiled metal clothes hanger. When my Father came down to visit us from his home in northern New Mexico, he'd put his laundry, without the benefit of laundry baskets, or plastic or paper bags, into the back of that disreputable-looking old boat of his. His clothing lay among dusty and greasy Beer Nuts bags, empty chocolate milk cartons and assorted plastic pimento sandwich containers. A loose wrench might float around next to my Father's work files. The car was a mess.

Daddy would arrive home, greeted by the usual celebratory meal, tacos, frijoles, arroz y calabacita. He would stay a few days and then he would leave— clothes washed, pressed, and neatly folded and placed in large paper bags in Jaws' back seat, the car cleaned and vacuumed, not an empty milk container to be found, all signs of his other volatile life removed.

Daddy would leave with a large plastic bag of toilet paper, my Mother's signature parting gift to anyone she truly loved; plates of food, including tacos; and his beloved Pasta in containers on the front seat.

My Father was the northern wind that occasionally blew south, always chilling my Mother's heart. He was her special boy, her rebellious, always truant lover boy. She was crazy about him and never really got over him.

Although my Father had remarried after his divorce from my Mother, she would hear nothing of any possible romance for herself. She was a one-man woman. Or in her case, a two-man woman who only had one man at a time. After Tiburcio Faver died and E. E. Chávez blew into and out of her life, the far west and southern winds turned cold, very cold, and she came to rely on another man, God. The two husbands were both gone and couldn't give her what she always wanted—a gracious, loving, warm home, with a family that loved each other fiercely.

My older sister, Faride, married at eighteen and left home, moving to various places including Colorado. She grew up among Anglos and learned their ways. What my Mother created for my younger sister, Margo, and me, was a safe harbor, a home filled with tacos, hard work, prayer and expectation. Our hopes lay in the dream of my missing Father E. E. C.'s return. We all hung on to that inchoate dream. We wanted so hard for it to come true. We wanted to see our Mother happy, at last. But, alas, her happiness was never to be.

———

Between those celebratory taco visits, my Father's health deteriorated. He always drank heavily and he would often arrive with bloodshot eyes, old scabs and cuts on his face, bruises on his arms and another dent in Jaws. He got into scrapes we did-n't know about and a few we did.

On one of his visits he drove down with a friend, another alcoholic. They were both quite drunk, and I understand they stopped in bars from Santa Fe to just out-side Las Cruces. Mother was expecting Mr. C., and a sixth or seventh or tenth sense told her all was not well. When she heard an ambulance and then a police siren, she set off to the hospital. The driver of the vehicle died, but my Father lived. Daddy moved back to live with us for a while and my Mother dutifully took care of him for months as he recovered. He had had another bad accident years earlier, where his ribs were broken and his knee was shattered.

I remember my Father's accident; I remember the tragic death of his friend that night they were drinking heavily. Throughout the world, descansos/death markers by the side of the road pinpoint the spots where people have died. There are often one or more crosses to mark the spot, giving testimony to the tragic passage by vio-lence. Car bumpers can sometimes be seen nailed to a crucifix, or a baby's toy, as well as homemade signs and ironwork. The range of creativity is incredible. They honor those who have lost their lives on the road. New Mexico, Arizona, Texas and California are full of descansos, as are other U.S. states. You can find descansos in any part of the world, really.

This terrible event in my Father's life not only damaged him, but us as well.

IN A SPEEDING CAR

In a speeding car
At night
All those faces come to mind
People who've died by the road

They'd been friends for years
Drinking buddies
They knew each other in the north
Where they worked

They were both mid-fifties
Alcoholics

They drove south to visit family
Stopping here and there
To have a drink

Bill Skoch was at the wheel
His car a Volkswagen
Tiny crackerbox
Piece of shit

My Mother heard the ambulance
Something in her rose up
She just knew—
Something had kept them

Without thinking
She drove to the hospital
Arriving before the ambulance
Bill was dead
My Father was very drunk
Not aware of what was going on

Drunks are protected
By their drunkenness
From so many things

Bill came from a good Catholic family
All taught to forgive
His brother was the president of a bank

There was awkwardness
When Mother went to the bank
To ask for loans
She had to—on her teacher's salary
She couldn't make it alone

Mr. Skoch was kind to her
They prayed
Resolved things in their own way
But neither of them ever forgot

In a speeding car
At night
All those faces come to mind
People who've died by the road

My Father's drinking caused him to live a violent life. Years later, when he moved to Albuquerque from Santa Fe, he was mugged behind a popular eating place on Central Avenue.

Over the years his drinking worsened and caused him throat problems. It began with sputtering coughs and difficulty swallowing. I dreaded eating with him and planned my meals for later times if I could. It wasn't always possible, and my Mother knew my distress. Toward the latter part of his life, Mother was the one who sat with him as he laboriously worked his way through a meal of "soft tacos," frijoles, arroz and calabacita. Although he didn't really like beans, calling them "poor people's food," he would occasionally eat my Mother's tasty frijoles. Daddy loved Mother's calabacita, her homemade squash casserole that she always prepared "just for him."

I dreaded eating with my Father in public places. Once in a Luby's cafeteria he nearly choked to death. His face turned red, then purple. Much to his chagrin and visible anger, I yelled out to anyone within earshot, "Can anyone help us?"

I hadn't known what to do. My Father gave me a dark look, stormed off toward the men's room and returned half an hour later, composed but angry.

I think my outcry jolted him back from the precipice somehow. I like to think so, because I was terrified. My constant prayer those last fifteen years of my Father's life when he lived next door to me as my neighbor and vecino, my most heartfelt prayer and plea to God was that Mr. C. wouldn't choke to death. To me, it was such an ignominious death, so unbefitting my Father's intelligence and will.

Throughout all those years there were many scares, frantic races to the hospital in too many ambulances, various near-death moments, but despite constant worry, he never did choke to death. I am grateful to God for that.

I can see my Father at my Mother's abundant Taco Table. She talks to him softly, but not too much. She lets him eat slowly. He takes his time, chewing his food well, although he always puts too much food in his mouth. Sometimes he has to spit it out. And sometimes he excuses himself to go to the bathroom to cough or throw up.

My Mother is patient. She loves the old rascal. And he should know it by now.

Calabacita Ernesto

(Pa' Mi Viejito)

6 smallish zucchini squash, diced

6 pattypan squash, diced

1 small onion

Cooking oil, as needed

2 cloves garlic, chopped

3 ears corn, boiled and cut from cobs

½ cup milk

Salt to taste

1 tablespoon comino/ground cumin

Monterey Jack cheese

Cut squash into medium-sized pieces. Sauté with small onion. Add garlic.

Set aside. You can also steam the squash and onion if you prefer. I prefer to steam the squash and onion as I like a softer texture, but it's also very tasty to sauté the squash.

The dish can be made with only zucchini or, for variety, you can add patty-pan. It makes a nice mix.

Either way, combine onion, garlic and squash. Add fresh corn kernels to mixture. There is nothing like fresh corn in Calabacita. You can use a can of corn, but why?

Simmer with a little milk to moisten. Add salt to taste. Add comino. Gently simmer. Add cheese at the end and cover to melt the cheese.

You can also bake Calabacita at 350 degrees F until it bubbles, about half an hour.

Enjoy this wonderful dish. And when you do, send a prayerful hello to Mr. C.

Midnight Rides and a Set of Nasty-Looking False Teeth

Tacos have so permeated my life, I don't know where one taco story ends and another begins. Once I was relating what I thought of as my dream, only to realize I had appropriated my younger sister Margo's dream.

"Denise," she said reproachfully, "that's my dream!"

If my sisters were to write their taco stories, their own taco testimonies, they might be similar to mine, but also very different. There would be stories that would connect and divide. One might agregarle un poco, add on a bit more, or leave something out. One might add a forgotten detail or expound on some forgotten taco insight. My sister Margo and I have always wanted to write a joint collection of stories on the same themes but from different perspectives. She remembers the salads. I can't remember lettuce being part of my life. I remember entering any number of dimly lit bars looking for my Father, my Mother having sent me in to plead with him to come home. Thank God my sister doesn't remember that.

We both remember driving around town in our pajamas looking for my Father, driving on Picacho Street to see if he was in a motel on the east side of town, the area people called Little Oklahoma, with its used furniture and secondhand stores, its small tucked-away motels.

I am grateful to my cousin Fred Chilton for bringing my Father from his favorite drinking hole, the Welcome Inn, to attend his mother Granma Lupe's funeral. He saved me from the awful task of coaxing my Father out of the bar and sobering him up to go to the mortuary for the service.

And you know—what followed were tacos. Enormous amounts of food at my Aunt Elsie's house: red and green enchiladas, steaming Crock-Pots full of beans, mounded bowls of Spanish—really Mexican—rice, calabacita made the gringo way, not my Mother's way, ham, turkey, tacos in trays, folded tacos, baked green beans with crispy onion rings from the can, baked sweet potatoes with melted drizzled marshmallows, various types of coleslaw, white and yellow potato salad, store-bought dinner rolls and bolillos from Luján's Mexican bakery, and warm local tortillas. The list goes on and on. And this doesn't cover the desserts: all kinds of cakes, pies, pan dulce. We consoled one another and mourned my grandmother with food. She was 99.9 years of age, and while we ate we remembered Granma and her antics. She was terrified by her birthday cake, a wall of burning candles that leapt toward the sky, and she had a predilection for playing with windup toys. During the course of the funeral Mass my Father sobered up. It was a typical Chávez funeral, taco-filled and frisky.

When people gave my Father the pésame, he was leaden. In monosyllabic phrases he thanked them for coming. His long exhalations of air belied the state of his drunkenness. He was in a state of shock and unable to mourn. He never cried, never shared his sorrows with anyone. I never saw him cry for either his mother or mine.

When my Mother was dying, my Father hardly spoke as well. My Mother, when she could talk, accused him of avoiding her. She was angry and he knew it. As she got quieter and sicker, so did he. That last week he was in the room every day, and although I don't remember him crying, I saw his body shrink, until he became as small as I'd ever seen him. He was never a big man, although in the old pictures he looks tall and masculine with a broad chest. In my Mother's hospital room he looked like a displaced bird, all eyes and head. Who would take care of him, dote on him, call him sweetheart and make him Pasta and tacos? Who would buy his toilet paper and clean out his car and his apartment and do his laundry?

It was with some horror and dismay that I realized that I had become my Father's designated caregiver. My Mother had tried to shield me from that responsibility as long as she could, but eventually his illness broke her. She sat with him at the Taco Table and soothed him. She knew I found his choking disturbing. And sad to say, it gave me asco. His coughing fits repulsed me. I tried never to watch him eat.

Who then was the chosen one? I looked around and saw that it was me.

It was me, of course, always had been me. How could I have been so blind? I knew there was no getting away from it. I gathered up everything I owned, which was very little, and moved from Santa Fe back to Las Cruces. The most burdensome thing in my life at that time was a greasy old stove. Daniel packed everything up for me. He was unhappy that I was moving and he didn't personally want to move. That first year was rough. Daniel liked Santa Fe and didn't have any friends in Las Cruces, no life at all. He was a sculptor and jewelry designer and was told by a local art doyenne to make it "bigger and more Western." What hopes did he have in a town with such limited vision?

———◦•◦•◦———

Daddy was cantankerous, out of control, and seemed to be drinking more than before. He was unraveling in front of me. He would call to tell me he'd lost his keys, his car, and once, his false teeth. I was happy to help him get a new set of teeth from a nearby dentist who had his office conveniently at the end of the street. Doctor Franco came over and did all the prep work and ¡zas! the new teeth were in and they were beautiful! Those ugly dark yellow fangs of Daddy's used to be the bane of my Mother's existence.

"Can't you tell your Dad about his teeth?" she used to ask with exasperation.

Hell no, I couldn't. No one could. He got them in Juárez from Dr. Cut 'Em or Dr. Quack or Dr. Fulano de Tal. There was no telling Mr. C. that his cheap false teeth were just that, cheap and ugly as hell. The two front teeth had a terrible over-bite and hung below his lower lip. Hell, who could say anything about those teeth? I remember dancing with my Father once at a wedding. We got trapped dancing an interminable wedding march and were forced to see it through. He

smiled up at me with those fangs of his. I felt a terrible sad love for him. He wasn't
a good dancer, his steps were small and unsure, but he gave it all he could.

ON MEETING YOU IN DREAM AND REMEMBERING OUR DANCE

His little legs, dancing, dancing
The corrida
Run-racing
Against rice-twisted floor.

There is a rhythm in this dance
A sense of bandy-legged pride,
Father, an ill placed longing
For your sweetened flesh,
Lost stories.

They don't know, look at them,
They don't have the hop,
The salt of joy, you know,
The desire of this dance, Father.

She's the bride, my cousin
Her Father, George's brother,
My grandmother, George
George on the dollar
Yes, she looks that way, browned.

This family, sectioned
Creates wholes across desert landscape

Escape from
Escape from family—
You cannot

They are a part of your dreams
You find yourself loving them as you do
That state of wandering through rooms you know
Like your Father's face
His horseteeth not quite short enough
But who can say:
E. E.!
Or those damn Mexican teeth look like hell
What's wrong with you, anyway?

His little legs, dancing, dancing
Shuffle along
Your sad body in step as best you can
Dearly
Childfeet and flowing
The sails of your legs in cloth
Racing to be done.

His little legs
Dancing
Dancing.

With my Father's new smile began fifteen years of hard work for both of us.

Toward the end of that first year my Father was beaten, by whom I am not sure. Where, it's also hard to say. He had started the night at the Welcome Inn, his favorite hangout, but he seemed to end up somewhere else. In snatches he told me about a man, a place. The horror of that night never left him. He was frightened for years, and in bits and pieces of nightmare moments, he tried to relate the events of that time to me. I could never put it all together and I didn't want to. He was still very scared and kept asking me if he was safe. Yes, I'd say, no one is coming to get you. I often had to console him and tell him he was home and that everything was all right.

Prior to this cataclysmic event, Daddy had gone on raving drunks, and one night, when I was home, he banged on the door for me to let him in. It was after two in the morning, that alcoholic witching hour. He was incoherent, his voice thick, slurred, evil. I heard a demon inside of him and yelled back, "I can't let you in. I'm sorry, Daddy. Go home. Go to bed. Rest."

He beat on the door for a long time, cursed me and all the generations of people named Chávez. He finally took off down the street, hopefully to his place two houses away. I stood on the other side of that too-thin wooden door with its trinity of windows peering out into the ghostly darkness and prayed he wouldn't return. It broke my heart to refuse him entry. But I knew no good would come of that possible encounter. He was not himself.

I knew that fiendish voice, having heard it once before outside my house in Santa Fe. A woman foamed and raved outside my bedroom as darkness moved and then spoke through her. I could sense her inexplicable anguish. All I can say is that I knew she was possessed. That heavy, sodden tongue had now taken hold of my Father. I couldn't bear to look at him, much less let him into the house. I was sorry but it couldn't be. He would turn abusive if he wasn't already, and he might hurt himself or me. I was alone in the house and knew I couldn't deal with his strength.

As an older man he was thin but strong. More than once he would fall to the floor in a weakened state and it took several caregivers to lift him up. I knew I couldn't lift him up or carry him anywhere. And who knew what horrible words he would have spouted then in his rage and fury? Oh, no! He might have been my Father, he was, but he was not to be let in the house. He was very sick, and I was afraid of what he might do or become in front of me. Other times, I'd put him to bed, but this time I couldn't.

Eventually, I knew my Father's alcoholic luck would run out. I dreaded the scene in my mind. Anyone connected to an alcoholic knows that they will ultimately have to confront their mortality in one hard way or another. I played the scene in my mind more than once: I would find him in a pool of blood, unconscious or dead. When the time finally came, I found him thrown on the living room couch, bleeding from the head. Someone had taken a blunt instrument and shattered his skull, and there was an indentation on the right side of his head. He was in and out of consciousness, and despite this, he didn't want me to call the ambulance.

So we began our new lives together: me as caregiver, him as the one cared for. I became his mother and he my son. He was the child I never had, and for fifteen years the only diapers I changed were his. He was the child I never knew I would have and would learn to love deeply and care for. He was my Father and I was his everything.

So began the history of our new lives: daughter/father/neighbors/friends/and yes, sometimes enemies.

The story of those fifteen years would require another book. But be sure that tacos were always involved.

Oatmeal

Oatmeal. The word conjures up images of a past defined and inspired by food: easy food, healthy food, comfort food, just plain good and wonderful food.

Alas, for me, oatmeal was none of these things.

I have visions of my Mother rushing off to teach school in the mornings—but before that, there was her daily duty, our morning oatmeal. Between getting ready for work, helping us to get ourselves ready and catching snatches of her second news program for the day, the first having been an hour earlier, Mother attempted to clean up the house a little bit as she dumped several cups of oatmeal into a pan of water.

She never got back to the pan until the oatmeal had overflowed, was burned or ran out of water. If the oatmeal needed more water, she would add a cup of cold water, stir the mash a bit and then put it back on the gas burner. Mother didn't believe in cooking slow. High heat was her only setting.

The oatmeal never had a smooth texture, ever. It was usually overcooked, lumpy and slightly burnt. The lumps would make us gag. No amount of sugar or honey helped. The taste was always bland, there was no separating individual grains; they all clumped together into some horrible mash. The shiny grey mush that Mother doled out to us from a large metal spoon was totally inedible.

Mother was organized and methodical, brilliant in her execution of all things having to do with her job—except of course when it came to cooking anything other than Mexican food. She would forget what she was doing and often wandered into the kitchen to find a cow's tongue shrunk to a miniaturized morsel, a steak charred or vegetables dissolved into pulp. She set fire to pans full of grease and blackened the interior of the house more than once. She was forever placing lemons all over the house, in corners, on tables and in piles in bowls, alleviating the burnt smell with the sharp pungency of the lemons that absorbed the smell of smoke.

———◦◦◦◦———

For years I couldn't tolerate oatmeal. Gradually I learned to appreciate the grace and calm with which one could cook it. I also learned the true taste of that special food. I do eat oatmeal often now, especially in winter, but when we were young, my sister and I left it untouched. The soggy, wet mess that clumped together and called itself oatmeal nauseated us. On eating it, we had an overriding urge to throw up.

Some years ago, I fixed some for my sister, Margo.

"Is this what oatmeal is like?" she said.

"Yes, I know," I replied, "that's how it's supposed to taste."

"I can't believe it," my sister moaned. "Mother's was so bad! It was so lumpy I could never eat it."

A silence came over us as we thought of our Mother, who always fixed us oatmeal and then ran off to school. She was a woman who stood all day with her badly varicosed legs throbbing in pain, who monitored young children in dusty playgrounds and in cafeteria lines, who taught her charges love and respect for each other. She was a single mother who was always waiting for the child support check to come in the mail. And yet my sister and I were dressed well, we never lacked for anything we really needed. Our Mother always had money and treats for us, for all her children.

We remembered when the first Chinese restaurant, the China Temple, came to town. The three of us so wanted to try it out. All we'd ever eaten was canned Chun King chow mein. We relished it, of course, and wondered how anything could be better. One day, as a treat to us, my Mother dropped us off at the restaurant. Handing us some money, she told us to call her when we were finished eating.

Years later, I asked her why she hadn't gone with us that day, and she replied that there wasn't enough money for all of us to eat there. As a matter of fact, she admitted she'd never eaten at the China Temple. Feeling guilty, I resolved to take her there to eat, but I never did. I can't look at a can of Chun King without thinking of my Mother and her love of the chicken chow mein dinner. I don't think she ever ate in a real Chinese restaurant.

As we grew older, we still didn't have much money, but when we did, we would take Mother to eat oysters. It was a longstanding ritual every time the three of us would get together. There was only one place in town to go then to eat seafood. Ceremoniously we would escort Mother there, perhaps on a Sunday. After perusing the menu for a long time, she would order fried oysters.

Mother's eyes would mist over as we sat waiting for her oysters to arrive. She would once again tell us the story of her honeymoon in El Paso, of her life with her first husband, Tiburcio "Bucho" Faver. We would sit with rapt attention, wanting to know more about Mother's other/Texas life. That other life of hers seemed far away, as secret as the wedding photograph she kept at the back of her closet. She kept it hidden all the years she was married to my Father. It was a photo taken on her wedding day to Bucho Faver. Mother was in her mid-twenties; her hair was short and curly. Bucho was a little older. They were a handsome couple, thin, young, with rosy, hand-painted cheeks. In the photo, they stand proudly in front of a dramatic stairway, in what seems to be a large, high-ceilinged room. It turns out it was only a backdrop, and their marriage was to last a very short time. I could never imagine her as that young woman. I knew her as an older woman with long black hair in an elegant bun. I was used to seeing her struggling with another man, my Father.

I could never understand why my Mother kept the photograph in her closet, behind all her clothing and shoes. I realize now she did it in deference to my Father, out of respect to him and their marriage.

I can still see that wedding picture. Try as hard as I did those years I was growing up, I never found out who the man was in the photo. It never occurred to me to ask Mother. If she had wanted to put the photo on display, she would have. The fact that it was placed at the back of the closet signified it was a hidden part of her life, a personal thing we should not discuss.

"Bucho was so nice," Mother used to say. "He was so neat, so clean, he used to bathe three and four times a day. And he would change his shirt every time. He was always changing shirts. He asked me often to scrub his back in the bathtub, but I refused. I was too shy. How I wish I could go back and scrub his back now. He was a good man. He was so nice to me. He would say, 'Fina,' that was his nickname for me, Fina, 'you'll never have to work. I'll take care of you all the days of your life.'"

By this point in the story, the oysters would arrive and I would be transported again to El Paso, the seafood restaurant on Mesa Street, the place they ate every night on their honeymoon. I saw Mother's bright lovely face, her shining, loose, short hair, the handsome seriousness of her new husband; I felt the joy and love of those days of novelty and delight.

Mother ate her oysters slowly, silently. She winced a bit with each bite, almost with a certain familiar distaste. I don't think she really liked the taste of oysters, fried or unfried.

I never tired of Mother's story about the oysters and El Paso. Whenever I took her out to eat, I always encouraged her to order oysters. She began her story again where she'd left off, each account a little more detailed, a little sadder. Without pretension or illusion, Mother would begin anew the story of that long-ago time of hers—that time of oysters and love.

The story of the oysters was a sweet ritual to me, without room for surprise, until the year Mother told me the story of Bucho's death. That telling took years. I believe she waited until I could understand what it was to really love. And I don't think she would have told me the story if it hadn't been the exact day of the anniversary of his death. All the circumstances were right.

Mother and I sat in a parked car, on a moon-filled night, waiting for an attendant to open up a storage unit for us. It was the same place she stored a wooden chest that relatives from Texas had sent—a chest that used to belong to my Mother when she was married to Bucho. Mother started to cry softly as she told me it was the anniversary of Bucho's death.

The story that unraveled during that interminable wait detailed the onset of Bucho's illness. In her mother-in-law Mamá Gumersinda's house, Mother lay in her bed giving birth while Bucho was dying across the courtyard. Neither one could get close to the other.

———•·•·•———

Ay, food brings to mind family. If I could sum everything up I would toast our family and say thank you for the good times and even the bad.

And of course, there was always oatmeal: the vision of my Mother coming home those days when she wasn't on lunch duty to check her mail. Foraging through the refrigerator, she would invariably find a container of cold oatmeal. She felt it was her duty to eat it and not let it go to waste despite the fact it was soggier, colder and lumpier than before.

Mother was a woman who never had time to eat a normal lunch. She was always too busy, on the go. And besides, all her children—and there were many of them—were waiting. After hastily downing her unsavory lunch of cold oatmeal, she would race back to school, grabbing the mail, mostly bills, and relieve us once again of our burden of leftover oatmeal.

My Mother didn't have time for cooking unless it was a special meal like tacos. Her staples were potted meat slapped into a tortilla, corned beef hash slapped into a tortilla, cheese slapped into a tortilla, pinto beans slapped into a tortilla, anything slapped into a tortilla, always with a side of green chile, or cottage cheese and canned peaches, or cans of unheated corn or peas or hominy, or corn flakes with low-fat milk. She usually ended her meals with something sweet, a dollop of jam or honey slapped into a tortilla.

———•·•·•———

Mother never talked about how bad off we really were or how she struggled with her debts. I remember her wooden desk piled high with bills she would pay off at the rate of five or ten dollars a month. She was always on the phone promising to do good by some creditor. Pasted on the base of her light fixture was the phrase, "Do I oppress others with my sense of gloom?"

Mother was full of plans, agendas and dreams. She wanted to paint the house or buy a new couch or make new curtains or go see her sister in El Polvo. She did her very best, but cooking and cleaning were never her priorities. If the house was untidy, she said it was because she either didn't have time or she didn't feel like it.

When you move fast, you can't monitor the lumps. What she got in her lifetime were oysters from one man, oatmeal from another. But she never despaired, or at least not for too long. In her world, those she loved were more important than anything else, and whatever they brought her, sorrow, joy or longing, she was up to the task. Mother was a woman who never had time to smell the roses. Yet she was the rose, unknown to herself.

Taco Times: Through Thick and Pretty Thin

Our college years were, for the most part, happy times for all of us, including my Mother. She wasn't happy at first that I had won a scholarship to major in drama when I was a senior in high school. I won the Best Actress award in a play called *Grey Bread*. The prize included a $200-a-year scholarship to New Mexico State University. It wasn't much, but it did help my Mother and she was grateful.

She was shocked to realize how much rehearsal time was involved. "What, another rehearsal?" I do think she grew to love the theatre as much as I did. What she didn't like were the late-night rehearsals, picking me up at 2 a.m. in front of the theatre because our Russian director, Hershel Zohn, was keeping us overtime yet another night. Another thing she didn't like were the men in the drama department, a bunch of loose libertines sin juicio, no judgment or morals at all.

I really didn't date until I was in college, and when I did, all hell broke loose, or so my Mother imagined. We would go drinking in Juárez, and sometimes I would come home drunk. The drink mixtures were really awful and consisted of all kinds of horrible combinations: Bloody Marys chased with Zombies, Rum and Cokes, Daiquiris and Grasshoppers followed by White Russians. It was a crazy time and everyone knew it. We all drank and smoked an occasional cigarette on the way back home from Juárez in the back seat of a car, all the girls clumped together to avoid our jerky dates. We all loved to dance, and so often my sister and I double dated and went dancing. Cousins and sisters went in groups, and in that there was safety.

My Mother worried and with cause, but for the most part, we were not without some scruples. Pregnancy was out, a taboo. Once my Mother came to me and told me solemnly that if I should ever get pregnant (I had no plans for it, I could have told her!) that I should never ever think of having an abortion. I appreciated my very Catholic, Mass-every-morning Mother telling me this. It gave me a reason to never get pregnant and made me understand that I was safe and loved, no matter what I ever did or whatever happened to me.

She also once made me promise I would never become an alcoholic. In later years when I worked as a cocktail waitress and drink-serving waitress it cured me of the need to drink. It is a terrible tragedy for so many people. I have seen the sadness up close, and when I walk by bars, I can't stand the smell. I still haven't been able to give up alcohol entirely, but someday, as a practioner of Buddhism, I will. I have seen the devastation that alcoholism causes and want to end our family dysfunction with my conscious release of alcohol.

THE FIFTH NOVICE PRECEPT IN BUDDHISM

Aware of the suffering caused by the consumption of alcohol, drugs and other intoxicants, I vow not to ingest any food or beverage that contains toxins and that deprives

*me of the control of my body and mind and brings about heaviness or ill-being in my
body or my spirit. I am determined to practice mindful eating, drinking and consum-
ing, to consume only items that bring peace and joy to my body and mind.*

My Mother always tried her best to make life very good for us. If she made me
promise not to drink, I understood her request. My Mother taught us to aim high in
all we did, to do our very best at all times and to have goals. She believed in us.
And her belief in us gave us the needed strength to believe in ourselves. She struggled hard to make us a family at all times.

Tacos were our measure of unity, our bond to who we were, what we believed.

In high school and college, I never thought of ordering tacos away from home;
they were never up to my standards. Sometimes we ate hamburgers, eight for a dollar, and that was a special treat. While Mother loved the hamburgers, she was
unhappy with the greasy, fingerprinted door to our favorite restaurant and mentioned it to the owner. That was her way: if something was not acceptable,
improper or out of order, she tried to fix it.

The only thing she couldn't fix was my Father. Nobody could fix him. The man
was unfixable, and the sooner you realized it, the better. It fell to me to try and fix
him. But despite the fact he couldn't walk without a walker in his later years and
had stopped drinking by default, he was still an alcoholic.

His voice boomed loud and strong, and he could be heard down the street curs-
ing one or another caregiver. My vecina, Ofelia Carrillo, knew how he was doing by
the timbre of his voice. If he wasn't yelling at someone, she knew he was ill. He was
abusive to the staff that took care of him, especially an occasional male nurse who
might be sent down from Respite Care. He thought all male nurses were homo-
sexuals. He had a fear of that for some reason, a volatile intolerance that, like his
racism, unnerved me. He could be nasty, rude and downright ugly, but never once
did he really complain about his health. He was saddened by it, dismayed, surprised at what had befallen him, but never once did he sound pitiful. He was a

proud man and bore his ill health with dignity, as his throat doctor introduced one and then another metal hose, of growing width, down his esophagus to open up the crabgrass of his throat. I never heard him complain about these sessions that for me were torture. He was brave, mi viejito.

Waves of sadness sometimes overwhelm me when I think of my parents' lives. Both of them wanted to be happy, but they could never be happy with one another. My Mother wanted a well-run home. My Father could never give her that. She wanted someone around to help her fix and take care of things, someone to mow the grass, repair the washer or dryer, someone to read the paper at the kitchen table with and someone to grow old with. My Father was a helpless, hapless individual. I don't think he ever learned how to use a washing machine. His apartments were always uninhabitable, and yet he took offense when I refused to drink from his glasses and cups or eat from his plates. I moved him lock, stock and barrel to different apartments over the years and cleaned up his mess and disorder so that he could get his deposits back. I learned much about him in those awful moves.

During one particularly harrowing move, my future husband, Daniel, and a friend agreed to move my Father's things in a borrowed truck. I'll never forget Daniel's look of sheer incredulity at the condition of my Father's kitchen. To his credit, he bit his lip and said nothing as we wrapped things up and boxed them. Daddy had cartons of old phonograph records and clothing in his closet, old cracked shoes from the 1950s, wide out-of-style ties, white belts and disco shirts with pointy collars. Daniel saw the worst of my Father and said little.

I had offered to clean the apartment and later rued my goodwill. I doubted Daddy would get his deposit back. I slaved in his dungeon of a one-bedroom apartment for several days. He'd disappear early, return late. He'd appear around lunchtime with a hamburger or some tacos. At night he took me out to eat seafood or pizza at Jack's Lounge on Central Avenue, his Albuquerque watering hole. Days with my Father, ay! Days with my Mother, ay! Days of many, many tacos, ay!

Questions Left Unanswered

I always wanted to talk to my Father about my Mother. I often wanted to ask him if he loved her. Or maybe I knew he did love her, but not how much. I respected his privacy and understood that he could never live with her and drink. And he also loved women, never wanted to stop loving women. Mother would never tolerate that. And she would embarrass him. And that was unforgivable, above all things. He didn't like drama, other people's dramas, especially my Mother's ongoing endless dramas, he only liked his own.

There were so many things I wanted to ask him. I wish I had on our many drives on the back road to El Paso, Texas, going south on Highway 28, his favorite drive in the world, mine as well, the two of us eating frozen yoghurt, me giving him his history tape, reminding him who had died, who lived where and what had happened to so and so and so and so. My Father lived his only freedom those last years of his life either in a speeding car in the shadows of trees in the world's largest pecan orchard, a place of solace and growth, or in his dreams. I wanted to ask him so many things, but I didn't want to take away his hope, whatever it was. I felt asking him about things he wanted to forget would somehow hurt or diminish him. How I wish I had asked the questions!

I wish, too, that I could ask my Mother questions: mostly about Tiburcio Faver and how she came to know him and love him and then how she felt about her two husbands in her later years. What can you tell me about them? And which one did you love more? And please, how do you make your rice so good? And what are the ingredients to your tortilla masa that became your pan that became your sopaipillas? I can see you making the masa but I am distracted by other things. Life was moving too fast and before I knew it, it changed. What happened to all the recipes for food and living? What happened to them? And after all this time, who cares, who really cares about Granma Lupe's Pasta or your tacos, Mrs. C.?

The Chicken Lady

In my thoughts I often find myself in Pátzcuaro, México. The familiar food vendor, "the chicken lady," sells her delicious roasted chicken tacos from her small puesto on the central plaza. At her colorful traveling cart she flips homemade corn tortillas into a red chile sauce. Her arms are covered in red chile up to her elbows. Without thinking, she will add a few gnarly chicken feet to your already full plate, as a special treat.

Nearby, mujeres indígenas, native women, ply their wares. One day I had one of them braid my hair with their traditional black yarn hair ornaments. Another time one of them asked me if I had any children.

"No," I replied.

"Qué lástima," she answered, "but not to worry, I know someone who can fix that."

"Not now. Perhaps later," I said, with trepidation, wanting to go with her, but afraid.

Alas, I never made that trip to the local curandera to have her pray over me, give me a limpia, a cleansing ritual to make my womb fertile. Now, after all these years, the aroma of roasted chicken tacos con chile colorado reminds me of Pátzcuaro, Michoacán, México.

To me, it will always be a place of magic, lost children.

Manteca Vieja

Sylvia Bejarano, a salesperson at the local Hertz Rent A Car at the Hilton Hotel in Las Cruces, sees me fairly often and asks me what I have been working on.

"A book on tacos," I tell her.

"Tacos? Tacos!"

I knew that Sylvia would like the idea. There hasn't been one person who hasn't liked the idea of a book about tacos.

"I have the secret of good tacos," Sylvia said with surety.

"What's that?" I asked curiously.

"Manteca vieja," Sylvia said with delight and consummate understanding.

Manteca vieja? The phrase alone conjured up Mother's tinita, her silver metal grease container she always had on top of her stove. It held her leftover grease, the savory bacon drippings and tasty, congealed hamburger fat, and anything else that constituted re-usable oil.

I hadn't thought of my Mother's silver metal tinita in years. Years! It was always a little bit greasy on the outside, and when I did the dishes I always first wiped down the stove and then the tinita, carefully. I remembered how my Mother re-used her oil and fat. What ever happened to the tinita?

All these thoughts came to me in a sudden flash. Suddenly I was back in the basement of the Hilton filling out car rental information as Sylvia expounded on the merits of manteca vieja.

"If you want a really tasty taco, fry it in manteca vieja."

"Manteca vieja?"

"Tacos taste better cooked in manteca vieja, old oil. I keep it and use it all: bacon grease, taco grease, lard. It's good to use for tamales, you blend in the old oil for flavor. Be sure and skim the top."

I understood what she meant. Our Mothers knew the merit of saving this tasty grease and re-using it to savor our food. This manteca vieja went into the frijoles, the tamales and the stews.

I was a vegetarian for many years, still am in my mind, save for the occasional hot dog, hamburger, taco or the holy albóndigas, sacred meatballs, that our nearby pueblo of Tortugas makes each year and shares with the public for the feast day of Our Lady of Guadalupe.

In addition to these unparalleled meatballs, I will always eat my own tacos. I often eschew a hot dog or hamburger, nearly always avoid chicken and turkey, rarely can eat eggs ("too feather-y") and won't have anything to do with steaks—they have no allure for me—but a good taco is not to be passed up, especially if they are your own family's recipes and you knew the Madrina del Taco, La Mera Mera, the One and Only, and that woman happened to be your own Mother.

I believe Sylvia about the manteca vieja. Sadly, I think few people I know have a tinita of grease on their stove anymore. What happened to that tradition? Is saving manteca vieja a thing of the past? Do certain cultures save more grease and reuse it more than other cultures? I've been taught not to fear grease, and yet I've moved away from manteca vieja to my special health-food store canola oil.

I ponder the unspeakable. I've never saved any kind of grease, ever!

My husband, Daniel, likes to tell the story of one of our dates. It had to be one of our first dates, if not the first. I was living in Santa Fe then, and one night he came over. I reported to him that I had a clogged kitchen drain and I wondered if he could help me out. It never occurred to me that he was virtually a stranger and that I had no business asking for help of such a personal nature. But I did, and maybe this is what endeared me to him.

"Taco grease," I stated with absolute calm as he hunched down in front of the sink and started working on the clogged drainpipe.

"Taco grease? You put taco grease down the sink?" he said, only slightly raising his voice. He seemed relatively calm.

For some reason I had decided to throw the taco grease in the sink. Don't ask me why. I haven't done it since then.

"Yeah, taco grease," I said, apologetically. Cold taco grease converts into a nasty oily white film. No doubt some meat particles were stuck in there as well. I had assigned him an unpleasant task, but he was up to it. I liked that.

I appreciated the fact that the man didn't flinch when I reported the cause of the problem. Most men would have run then, but no, Daniel stayed and has continued to assist me in the many and myriad dramas of domestic life that have ensued over the years: countless mice and birds we've had to chase down in the middle of the groggy night, gifts from our two thoughtful cats; a visiting rat we could never catch that we named Rat-iel, an unwanted adoptee we came to know and love, who lived in our stove for several months and grew to gigantic proportions when I left bananas and nuts out for him "so he wouldn't starve"; an army of insects of all types and sizes that have wandered into our home and have been greeted with my ear-piercing screams: centipedes, worms, flying roaches, bees, and once, a bat that took shelter on the screen door to the back yard. We've had emergency fires and power outages, and once had to vacate our house for four days after a particularly virulent bug spraying rendered the house uninhabitable. I knew when I saw the bug man's hand with several missing fingers and several gnarled remaining claw-like digits that it was a bad omen to have called the exterminators.

We've had taco disasters and grease spillage; we've burned ourselves, but not too badly. My friend and fellow writer Melissa Flores told me about a friend of her mother's who survived a taco grease fire and still lives with badly scarred reddish arms. Consequently, Mrs. Flores rarely makes tacos and when she does, she leans out far and virtually flings the taco into the pan with the oil. I don't blame her.

THINGS THAT HAVE LEFT ME WITH LONGING

The memory of my Mother's arroz
The memory of my Mother's homemade pan
The memory of my Mother's fluffy sopaipillas
My memory of my Granma's Pasta as made by my Mother

UNANSWERED QUESTIONS

The Great Debate: the benefits of lard vs. cooking oil?
Rolled or folded?
Longhorn or Monterey Jack?
Red or green?

FOOD TABOOS

Overly aggressive mashing up of fried eggs
Too much pepper
Too much salt
Being ungracious and not hospitable to guests
Not feeding people when they're hungry
Food snobbery
Choking while eating
Talking while eating
Not having enough food. Food was richness to my Mother. To have a refrigera-
   tor full of food and a new dress from the United Department Store was par-
   adise to her, a sign of sure wealth and abundant blessing.

Tacos after 50

I am now what you would call a mature woman. How mature I am, I am not really
sure. But I am older and I have learned a lot. There are many things I wish I'd done
but not too many. My life has been full of detail and the comfort of home. I like to
travel, but not too much. I'd rather be walking down my street than driving away.
I'd rather not step out the door but too often I have to. My life has become either

one of noisy service or a jealous quiet that I strive to preserve at all costs. I still wander through the familiar rooms of my Mother's house, but now I mostly do this in my mind, as I live a short ways down the street. Some years ago I bought another house at the end of the block and moved here after the washing machine's pipes froze one winter when I was away at a writer's retreat. It was a traumatic move leaving Mother's house for the big house down the street. I'm moving back. I have to. I can't stand being gone from the old house any longer. I need to get back to my old haunt, only there is so much work to do, I'll have to win the lottery to get things back in shape.

The latest news is that recently my husband cracked the blue window in the once Blue Room when he moved it to brace the wood that surrounded it.

At first I was very upset. But then I saw how upset he was. I think he'd waited several days to tell me, to find a right time to say that the window had cracked in one corner, the corner the workman had had to chip to fit the window in its place that first time. How could I be angry? Daniel looked so tired, so bereft. He suggested we integrate the old with the new. The window was mostly intact. We'd just put some stained glass on the outside, so that when we moved back home—and we would—we would integrate the old with the new. It sounded like a good idea. And besides, what could we do?

The window had cracked. It happened, just like that, and there was no going back. Ni modo. I mourned—but not too long—the window that was in the Blue Room, my Mother's blue window. It was ruined, but not really. It would be a different window from now on.

The last time I dreamt about my Mother she saved me from the end-of-the-world destruction that I often dream about. Usually there is a terrible flood that overtakes the world, and I am climbing a large mountain to get away. In the distance, a wall of water devastates the land and all life there. Mother has pulled me to safety once again, and with a sudden realization, I understand that she has brought me to her home. The small but lovely place is set on a high hill near the sky. From there she can look down on the world of men and women. Mother is somewhat embarrassed that I have finally found her at home. She has eluded me for many years, but now I have seen where she lives. I approve. It is a beautiful faraway place, and it is unlikely that I will visit it again for some time. And that's all right, I know where she is now.

———•◦•◦•———

I've had many blessings: a fine Mother, a really dear Father, who despite his illness, was always loving to me. I hadn't planned on being the one to take care of my Father and to carry on my Mother's taco legacy, but there you have it. Someone had to step forward and roll the cara side in.

I remember the people who came to my Mother's Taco Table, my parents' friends, many now deceased, my sisters, their friends, my friends, classmates, hundreds of people who over the years enjoyed tacos during the many nights at the round table. Now very few people come to my house, the few and select, few relatives. The older I have become, the more reclusive I am. No one comes to see me, and if they come unannounced, I am always surprised. With Mother, it was the opposite. She loved company, and there was always room for more. Delfina, ¡más tacos!! I have become isolated from family, more accessible to the world, but to my own kin, I am sometimes a stranger. It saddens me. How to seek my way out of this isolation? Tacos can assist. And so can beans.

Your Basic Bean Recipe

2 pounds uncooked pinto beans

A large Crock-Pot or cooker or beloved olla. Don't cook the beans in a cooker that is too small. They need room to expand and tenderize. The longer you can cook the beans, the better. Simmer your way to heaven. And a soft pinto bean, cooked just right, IS heaven. Most people cook beans too fast. You can tell an undercooked bean on first bite as the skins are hard and the bean has no integrity.

Water, as needed

1 large onion

Meat for flavor: this could include a ham bone, salt pork, bacon or a dollop of manteca vieja.

Salt to taste

Cooking oil

Wash beans well. Separate dry "floaters" and the old veteranos who are black. Clear out the flotsam, which will include bean husks and small rocks. Don't act surprised—yes, rocks. Try and buy local beans from this year's crop; it really makes a difference.

Once beans are assessed and cleaned, put them in a Crock-Pot and cover with water. Add onion for taste or meat if you want that seasoning of bacon or pork. Cook most of the day or sometimes all night on low heat. As long as you have enough water in the Crock-Pot you can cook the beans all night. There is nothing like the smell of a fresh pot of beans. Forget the smell of early-morning coffee; learn to wake up to early-morning beans!

Save the salt addition till the very end; beans will cook faster without the added salt.

Once the beans are cooked, set aside. Put oil in the sartén and heat to high. Place a cupful of beans in the sartén to "güiso." A lovely cloud of steamy bean heat will rise skyward and you will know that you have done the güiso correctly.

Many people don't know that the güiso stage of cooking adds a caramelized topping and incredibly delicate and lovely flavor to beans. You don't have to güiso all the beans at once; güiso as you need beans. Once a batch of beans has been güiso-ed, they will blend with their other friends and provide you with a wonderfully rich batch of sweetly roasted caramelized beans, a la Mexicana!

The Memory of Tacos Past

Does one create memory from food, or does food create memory? Both are the case for me. I am indistinguishable from family, food and culture.

In the harsh times, I have longed for a good homemade taco, dreamed myself home, sitting in front of the windows in my Mother's dining room, at the Taco Table, as she serves her guests two and three tacos at a time, scooping them with a metal spatula and laying them flat on a waiting plate.

My sister Margo recalls the delicious time of putting on the cheese. This would be the final, sacred moment of taco completion.

I recall the rolling, rolling, rolling of the palotes, rolling pins of all sizes in our hands as we rolled out tortillas, Mother's pan or a sopaipilla. I remember the faces of the young and old who learned to make tortillas and tacos in my Mother's small humid kitchen. If you walked in while the taco process was taking place, you were likely to be drafted into service. Age didn't matter. Sex didn't matter. Ethnicity didn't matter.

With my Mother's taco work, all were equal. To her, a taco was wealth and health, far beyond the usual. A refrigerator full of food was the greatest blessing, and family and friends around to share those taco meals, well, surely this was her heaven.

My wish is that those who read this book will find in it something special. Who would have ever thought that a little 6 x 1-inch rolled taco could bring such solace? Thousands upon thousands of tacos were consumed in our little house. They came out of a small kitchen piping hot. They fed multitudes, or maybe it just seemed that way. They were prepared with love and maybe that's why they tasted so good.

Each of us has our tradition and culture and foods. My story is just one. It talks of two people with disparate lives who loved each other, one of them not enough, one of them too much, people who brought children into the world, who tried to reconcile the disparities but never were able to, people who argued, made up, forgave, avoided, forgot, remembered, were afraid to listen, knew the truth, but could never speak it aloud. They eventually forgave each other. These people were my parents. From them I have learned most of what I needed to know in this life. When I meditate deeply on their lives I always smile in gratitude.

I wish I could say they were happy people. They were and they weren't. I wish I could say they made peace with one another. They did and they didn't. If only … I could say, but I can't. They were the people they were and I have come to accept them. And I believe they have accepted me. We are complete now. He complido con ellos. I have completed with them. I am at peace. I was their daughter for better and often worse. And in that, too, I am at peace.

Recently I dreamed various women, ancestresses, were walking sideways in front of me. They had different bodies and shapes. I heard a voice say that there were seven of them. As they paraded in front of me, I knew they were and are my family of women, these seven ancestresses from different times and places.

Every one of them knew how to cook, of that I am sure. Some of them I have met, others I have yet to meet. But I am part of them and they are part of me. They know me. They are my family, my food, my culture. It's been a good life, a life surrounded by tacos.

LET'S HEAR IT FOR TACOS!

T is for Tacos
A is for awesome and you know it!
C is pa' la comida de mi gente
O is for ¡Órale!
S is for S, ¡Ese!

What does it spell?
T.A.C.O.S.
TACOS!

A Taco Testimony

I am no stranger to tacos. If I had to make a list of things I am familiar with, tacos would be high on the list, and for many reasons.

My Mother made sure that all the little kids, male and female, that passed through her house held a tiny rolling pin in their even tinier hands and made tortillas. I like the memory of my now oh-so-macho nephew at my Mother's table mastering the art.

As children, we were allowed to play on the kitchen floor with bandejas/pans of all shapes and sizes and with an odd assortment of lids Mother had accrued over the years. Very few lids ever had a matching pan, but somehow she partnered up the mismatched pieces and made a whole. Her old faithful frying pan, her beloved sartén, had a lid that fit perfectly, whether rice was simmering in there or a tasty pot roast.

Mother's foolproof theory was that young children should be kept low and occupied. And if they played on the kitchen floor it was good. No muss, no fuss.

Banging away, a one-person band on blue linoleum, or attempting to roll out a perfect round globe of misbehaving dough that insisted on becoming the island of Cuba, we were taught to be attentive to tortillas.

The mastery of making tortillas led, most naturally, to the mastery of taco production.

As a teenager, I'd sit at the dappled 1950s spotted red and white metal table rolling out taco after taco, overseen by Mother, who, vigilant as ever, made sure I didn't have the wrong side of the corn tortilla facing out.

For those who don't know, the cara side has more of a "burn factor" than the other side. The back side is less dark and is the side that should face out to greet the hungry world. Invariably, I had the wrong side facing out, much to my Mother's chagrin.

Mother often insisted that I re-roll. I would do so, with exasperation, eating taco meat from the bowl. Gingerly, or as best as I could, I redid the tacos, removing the taco meat that now lay smack dab in the middle of the cooling corn tortilla.

When we'd make tacos there were always two or three people rolling at a time. It might be that your fellow taco-roller would squeeze the meat into a little cylindrical shape, the meat ready to be inserted like a prefabricated mold. You had to move fast with hot tortillas and blistering taco meat. Most likely you kept a pan of cold water nearby to dip your fingers into when the heat got to be too much. There was an unspoken rule that you had to work fast—the imminent danger of badly burning your fingers on either the taco meat or hot tortillas always lurking. Have you ever had a taco-meat burn? It can really hurt. So many Mexican food injuries go unreported.

———•+•+•———

With tacos, as in life, there are unspoken rules:

CONSEJO

Remember that the more burnt side of the tortilla goes "in."

CONSEJO

Never have a dry meat base. Have you noticed that most tacos fall apart when you pick them up? This has to do with the lack of "binding." Mother taught us the art of moist tacos, adding in potatoes or some kind of vegetable that "holds" the meat together. The binding agent adds a moistness that is very desirable. Nothing is worse than either dry flyaway meat or greasy beadlets that leave a film on your upper palate.

CONSEJO

Don't forget to add onion. Garlic, as well, if you choose. And by all means, don't forget to include the comino/cumin seasoning. I can tell if a taco is superior three feet away by the glorious aroma of comino that wafts in my direction.

———•+•+•———

Observation #1. The folded taco had to have been invented in California, even though some say it comes from the Mexican state of Sonora or from Arizona. Who knows where all Mexican food mutations have come into being? No doubt the chimichanga was born there in a place with a strange name. The crisp half-shell tacos have become a favorite with Johnny-cook-'em-quicks. They probably have this type of taco at Mad Mex, a well-known Mexican restaurant in Pittsburgh that I recently discovered. I worry about restaurants with names like that and especially in places like Pittsburgh.

———•+•+•———

The rolled taco reached its pinnacle of greatness in my Mother's kitchen. Her neatly rolled tacos lay golden brown on an old familiar cookie sheet, a sheet that was never used for cookies other than biscochos. My Mother's tacos had a life and dignity of their own. They were perfectly symmetrical, resting contentedly with no loose meat hanging out to dry to a hard crisp, and Mother sprinkled two types of cheese on top. But first, the tacos went into a 350-degree oven to brown.

CONSEJO

Never put on the cheese too early.

CONSEJO

Watch what cheese you use. What happened to *cheese* cheese? Nowadays it's hard to find a decent cheese that melts the way it should. A combination of Longhorn and Monterey Jack works nicely.

CONSEJO

There's no getting away from frying the tortillas in oil. Sorry. It just won't taste the same. You can use low-fat oil. Canola oil works well. You can pat the tortilla dry, and this will help, but you can't take the grease away from the taco.

Observation #2. Many a taco or enchilada has been ruined by hypersensitivity to grease. You need a little grease to get the tortillas soft and pliable. Steaming them won't do. I nearly lost a friendship over a plate of steamed enchiladas once. So watch out!

There are so many things I love about where I live. One of them is those cultural givens that we take for granted, like Morrell lard. Las Cruces, New Mexico, is one of the few places that I've lived that has a run on Morrell lard each Christmas and at various other times throughout the year. I have driven across town and back again, in desperation, all hours of the day and night, searching for lard. Many of you have probably suffered the same fate. Lard is as necessary to us as air. There is no way you can make the perfect biscocho, our beloved sugar cookies—and I've tried—without lard.

I'll drive far for a taco. And as my husband says philosophically, "It's better to have tacos in times of no money than to have money and no tacos."

Tacos recall to me the special times: a house full of company of all ages, some little kid in the kitchen with a unisex apron around his neck like a giant bib, rolling out tortillas with a little rolling pin, another kid banging two mismatched lids together, pans strewn all over the floor, someone rolling tacos with an ouch! ouch! as they dip tender fingers into cold water. Someone nearby is checking the taco meat to see if it has enough salt, and someone else is frying up the tortillas while your cousin on your father's side grates cheese. In the background, someone yells, "¡Más tacos! More tacos!" as the kid with the lids—a future Ph.D.—begins a deafening drum roll on a metal pan. Nearby your nephew molds a fresh new world from what seems to be an inert and inanimate clump of dough.

Tacos. I know tacos. They are familiar. And not so ordinary.

P.S. I feel I have to put a disclaimer here. If you want to steam your tortillas, go ahead. Just see what you get.

DECLARATION TO THE UNIVERSE

My name is Denise Chávez.

I am fifty-seven years old.

My favorite food is Tacos.

My favorite colors are Purple and Red.

My secret ambition is to continue to be a writer.

Postre/Dessert

Marshmallow Surprise

I named this dessert after making it all these years without a name
because to eat it was and is always a comforting surprise.

1 bag small, white marshmallows

1 can pineapple pieces

2 cups chopped pecans

8 ounces whipping cream

Place marshmallows in a large bowl.

Drain pineapple juice and save for the Capirotada or Biscochos. Add the pineapple pieces to the marshmallows.

Add the chopped pecans.

Whip cream and fold into the marshmallows.

Mix all together. Chill.

Marshmallow Surprise really needs to be refrigerated for a while so the flavors blend.

It is a delicious dessert to eat any time, night or day. It will remind you of home and sitting in the darkness with only the Christmas tree lights on.

Biscochos
(A Special Festive Cookie)

1 pound pure lard (Morrell is good)

1 cup water or pineapple juice (for extra flavor)

1 cup sugar

1 tablespoon cinnamon

1 tablespoon anise seed (optional)

7–8 cups flour

Cinnamon and sugar mixture (for topping)

Cream the lard, add pineapple juice or water, and cream together until practically all of the liquid has been absorbed. Add sugar and cream the mixture until it is smooth. Add cinnamon and anise seed if you like it. Add flour until mixture is stiff enough to shape in the hand. Do not roll. Pat dough out to about ½ inch in thickness. Cut into small cookie shapes. Bake until brown, about 15 minutes, in a 350-degree F oven. Check that bottoms do not get burned. Sprinkle granulated sugar and cinnamon on top.

SEVERAL TIPS

• You cannot get away from using lard. Sorry! Crisco does not cut it.

• The pineapple juice adds a great flavor, but you can also use water or another juice; some people use wine. Depends on what you like.

• Watch to see that the biscochos do not cook too much. Take them out of the oven before you think they are done, as they can burn easily! The longer you have the oven on, the shorter time it takes to bake the cookies. This recipe will make about 6 dozen biscochos or more, depending on the size.

• The biscochos will keep a long time in the refrigerator. They are very popular at all times of the year, but during Christmas, they are extra special. You can't eat too many at once, but remember, a few go a long way!

Capirotada sin Vergüenza/Shameless Bread Pudding

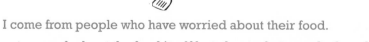

I come from people who have worried about their food.
Maybe not so much about the food itself but about what people thought

about their food. Our parents grew up hiding their bean and meat burritos in paper sacks. They've eaten their lunches away from others so they wouldn't be called poor Mexicans, beaners or mojados/wetbacks. Our parents were punished for speaking to each other in Spanish and for having an accent. This recipe for capirotada is without shame. It calls for what you have on hand without the need to get uptight for what you don't have.

1 loaf of old bread, white or whole wheat

Anything else that is bready and leftover—heck, throw in last week's flour tortillas!

Butter to coat pan

1 cup of raisins; old ones work just as well

1 cup of pecans, or any other kind of nuts you have on hand

Butter to spread in medium-sized dots on the bread

1 cup piloncillo/Mexican hard brown sugar, shredded from a cone, or brown sugar to taste

Pumpkin pie spice, cinnamon, or a combination of both

Water or juice to moisten bread; you can also use milk or wine if you choose. Some people use vegetable or meat broth. I'd stay away from the broth. This is a dessert dish, so go light on anything "meaty." The type of liquid depends on what you have and what you are feeling like that day. Use liquid to moisten bread but don't make it too soggy. You can always add liquid later.

1 cup of grated cheese or cheese slices, any kind and any shape that you have. This is your last chance to clean out your refrigerator of anything old or ugly that will soften up and taste good again!

Shred bread with your fingers. You can cut it if you choose, but why waste the time?

Place bread in a deep, buttered ovenproof dish.

Mix in raisins and nuts.

Dot with butter and piloncillo.

Sprinkle brown sugar and spices over the bread matter.

Add juice or liquid to taste.

Sprinkle or spread cheese on top.

Bake in a 350-degree F oven until it browns.

This dish is designed to be enjoyed on many levels. Not only is it easy to make, as well as tasty, but it makes you feel good because you can put anything you want into it and you don't have to explain anything to anyone.

Suggested things to put in: fruit of any kind, cottage cheese, yoghurt, chocolate chips. You get the idea.

Go ahead, be shameless!

Mejor Unos Tacos

My world begins when I open my front door. Out there—at any time of the day or night—I can find someone to help me scrub any ceiling or any floor of any room of my too-big house, prune or knock down a tree or cinder-block wall, cut the long overgrown grass that shouldn't be there in another year of drought or clean out a garage that holds too many un-necessary things—out there I can find someone, the right someone, to help me out in any way I want and need to be helped.

Some years back an older Mexicano man came to my front door looking for a pair of pants. How did he know I had a large black garbage bag full of my Father's sweat pants and soft cotton shirts in the back room? How did he know to come to my home looking for clothing? Was my house marked with an invisible sign, "Have shirts, have pants, know what it is to struggle, am willing to help?"

I know borders, real and imagined. I know what it is to have the rabia/anger, the unmitigated rage well up and then subside, wondering how I will enunciate my rights yet another time. Will I be waved away, dismissed or interrogated? "American citizen," I hear myself say in a faraway voice. "I am an American citizen."

There are so many things I hate about borders. I can't begin to articulate the disgust and sadness when I see the ever-changing sign at the immigration roadblock that tallies the yearly count, "1,457 alien removals." I hate the poverty and the class structure that causes men, women and children to cross the border in desperation. I hate the fact that young children have to sell packets of gum and myriad chucherías/junky trifles to tourists on the bridges, taking in car fumes. One day I saw a young boy high on fumes meander between cars in a stupor. I hate what is happening to the young women in Juárez and other border cities: the violations, the rapes, the deaths. Who is killing our daughters, our sisters, our cousins? And what about the young boy on the bridge? Who cares about him?

My borderland is a merciless and harsh desert with achingly blue skies. It can be and is a place of peaceful star-filled nights, wondrous nights that make you want to cry, they are so beautiful. And like so many things you come to love about a place or its people, they can break your heart.

The last image I have of that older Mexicano man was of him peering furtively down my small familiar street. You scared of my little street? Ay, señor, ¡no es posible! But it was.

The man had selected the best pair of pants from my plastic bag, no viejito "jump-up" sweat pants you just pull up fast, no güango, too-loose T-shirts, but my Father's beloved once-white best dress shirt.

The viejito could have been my Father. I was worried for him. Was the Migra nearby? Was he safe? Where was he headed? How long would it take him to get there, wherever he was going?

"Here's five dollars for some hamburgers," I said in Spanish with concern.

"Ay, señorita," he moaned, "por favor … mejor unos tacos."

Disdainfully, because I deserved his displeasure for having so much and understanding so little, he walked away, down the street, away from the purple-blue mountains, into the searing heat of that stark and vivid summer day.

Culture with a Capital C

Not a day goes by that I don't mourn the loss of something: the greenbelt around certain neighborhoods, a cotton field that has given way to a high-rise condominium, a family member who admits that she hates to read, the temporary loss of hope as a young cousin drops out of school to live with her boyfriend in an apartment her mother pays the rent for. What's wrong here?

I watch the news on television nightly, just as my Mother did, and can't understand why the world is at war. Would we be killing anyone at all if we knew who they really were, really knew who they were, knew their families, their culture, their food, their customs, their dreams, their lives?

The question, it seems to me, always comes down to Culture, with a capital C. If we weren't afraid of differences in language, food, customs and ways of living, would we be so insecure about our own selves?

The lack of Culture in contemporary society is manifest. It drives people to be intolerant, unsupportive and offensive. It allows people to hurt, maim and kill one another without reason.

I grew up thankfully with a Mother who taught me tolerance and love. I grew up with Culture, with books, and loved reading as a child. My Mother took us to movies and we attended the symphony. Mother was educated, cultured and very bright. But her understanding of Culture came not only from her education, but came from a greatness of heart. For without knowledge of the human heart, we can never be cultured people.

My Father taught me many things as well, but he was intolerant and unloving to most people. He was a good father to me despite the fact that he had many problems in his life to resolve. I know he loved me. And I loved him. My Father was a reader as well and was highly intelligent. His life was full of inappropriate actions and because of that, I can't say he was a cultured person. He and his wife Ruth once took me to a strip club, and I can tell you it was a terrible experience. I thought we were going out to dinner but instead I found myself trapped in a seedy nightclub, without a car or any means of escape, with the two of them, both drunk. I had no idea he was going to do this and I was mortified.

More than once I had the unpleasant task of being with my Father when he was drunk. I attribute his lack of good sense to his illness. He was missing essential parts of himself, and one of these was the appreciation of who and what he was, not only as a valuable human being but as a representative of his Culture. He had lost his self-worth somewhere along the way. He was a man that was deracinated, devoid of the pride of who he was. He was ashamed of being Mexican, of growing up on the east side of town, the poor side, and more than this, he was intolerant of his own people. How did this happen? Something was beaten out of him as a child and it never came back.

Although both my parents were very poor as children and came from places of great lack, my Mother was able to overcome the limitations of her landscape. I don't believe my Father ever was. And I attribute this eternal lack of his to the absence of Culture.

It's hard to understand how very poor both my parents' backgrounds were. If you travel to El Polvo, you will understand why it was called that. Originally the land there was given to Mexicanos to settle, and when the men went out to work early in the day they justifiably said they were headed toward "el polvo." Dust permeated every corner. If you went outside, you would have to dust yourself off. And keeping a house clean was hard.

Just don't use the phrase "el polvo" in Spain. "Hacer polvo" means to "have sex." I learned this during a Fullbright lecture series I gave some years back at various Spanish universities. I would mention to the students that I came from El Polvo and that I was headed back in that direction. I didn't know how true my statement was! It was an icebreaker, for sure, one I will never forget!

Life was very hard for my Mother and her family. A telling story is the one of Tía Pascualita, a woman who was so poor that she didn't get enough to eat during the Depression when she was pregnant with her child, Juanita.

MI TÍA PASCUALITA

Mi Tía Pascualita's world
Was never big enough
It was always crowded with the work of children

Juanita, particularly,
With her high-pitched, silly laughter
Her round little girl's face
That crazy toothless smile
Too wide for a woman of sixty

She was the retarded one
The one who never left home

Tía Pascualita was fair-skinned
With clear blue eyes
She was born to finer things
Than feeding chickens
Taking care of ragged children
And watering half-dead flowers in the sun

Texas: no place to live in the Depression
A place called El Polvo
The Dust

¿La Depresión?
Look at Juanita
That's what the Depression means to me—
Going on with what little I had
Because I had to—

I was pregnant then, never got to eat enough
Todavía me duele
It still hurts me
To know a child was starved in my womb

Now I'm old
It's comforting to have a daughter
One who will never leave home
¡Que Dios nos cuide!

¡Juanita!
Take the water can out
Give my plants all the water they want

Remember, m'ija
Cada cosa en este mundo tiene su trabajito
Each thing in this world has its work
Its reasons for going on

Each plant its hope for a tomorrow
Each rock its yearning for stillness
Each Mother a dream of peace
In a world with plenty of food

¡Ven! Patas Chuecas, you old twisted-footed rooster!
Y tu, Carmela, you fat thing
Greedier than all the rest
Isn't there ever enough for you?
What are you, selfish girl, a queen?
Take, take, take, giving nothing in return
Paco, Isidro y Claribel, yes, come my babies
Eat! Eat!
All you little fools, eat!

I have heard stories of my Father's family as well and the dire conditions under which they lived. My grandfather Epifanio Chávez would take off to do prospecting in the Organ Mountains or work elsewhere, often leaving his wife, Guadalupe, and their growing family. She suffered deeply and I often wonder if this wasn't why she was so cold, so intolerant of strangers.

Both my parents allowed me to see the world as it is and for that, I am grateful. There are stories yet untold about who these people were. My wish is to continue to write and publish the cuentos of these Río Grande families.

I have forgiven my Father and accepted the many good sides of his personality. And as my Father grew older and neared his death, he did expand as a human being and became a better person. We had many deep and valuable conversations, and he knew quite well how precious life was. I would say that he worked out his salvation on that rented hospital bed where he was taken care of for many years by so many people. He spent fifteen years in diapers, with little money and a mind that worked its way ever so slowly toward the light.

My Father eventually embraced his roots. He was very restless the night before he died. I called a priest to pray with us. As we prayed the rosary in Spanish, I could feel my Father relax and become peaceful. To hear the prayers in Spanish calmed him deeply. It is ironic and yet not so strange that the world he left behind so many years before came flooding back to him and was, at least, his deepest blessing and release. To embrace and to celebrate one's living and one's dying is the greatest known balm. In that long and terrible last night of his on earth, my Father found a deep peace.

Conversely, I have forgiven my Mother for her sometimes strange and distracted ways. She was dancing as fast as she could to make a home for us. It wasn't easy to be a single parent in the '50s, '60s and '70s. She never had good health and never really took care of herself. She and I had many battles, but we loved each other fiercely. We were both stubborn and sometimes intractable, dramatic and busy women, and yet I like to believe my Mother gave me her compassion and heart. I have forgiven her as I hope she has forgiven me of anything said or left unsaid or anything done or left undone.

As a result of who I am, where I live and how I have been taught to see and experience the world, I have continued my never-ending inquiry into the meaning and nature of Culture.

What is Culture? Synonyms for the word culture include: cultivation, refinement, taste, aestheticism, civilization, delicacy, breeding, schooling and grounding. We are taught to be cultured: well-bred, learned, educated, erudite, scholarly and tasteful. We are given tools to be a cultured person: we learn to read, to appreciate contemporary arts, to value history and to go to museums, the opera, ballet and the theatre. But Culture is more than a philosophy or diversion of the mind, it is an openness to experience, a willingness to accept the spirit and life of the Other through action and acceptance.

But still we are uncultured, and we continue to kill. And we continue to denigrate and shame others, to diminish their dreams, to refuse them rights we have ourselves. We look down on others who are less fortunate, less able to maintain the imagined life our greed dictates to us. We believe in holding them back, keeping them down, trapping them behind fences or putting them behind bars—or worse, we offer them little hope for achieving what for us is normal, expected.

I live very close to the U.S./México border, but you would think I lived on the moon. Many people here are afraid of Culture, afraid of what it means: having to meet other nationalities, most especially Mexicans and Native people, as equals.

How can someone who has lived here all his or her life not know at least a little Spanish or understand relevant cultural icons or tenets of belief? How long should it take for someone to take an interest in their environment and begin to understand the very basic realities of one's home place? There are those who readily embrace a Culture and those who keep themselves apart. How do we learn this separation? Who teaches us? Is it our parents, our family, our teachers, our friends?

I find myself saying over and over again, "It's a lack of Culture. People don't have Culture. They don't want to understand the Culture." But it's more than my simplistic pronouncements. All our life we are learning Culture and how to embrace life of all kinds and at all levels.

I was criticized for dressing my elderly Father in guayaberas, the loose and comfortable men's shirts. "He looks too Mexican," a relative complained. My response to that was that he *was* a Mexican! And for anyone's information, the guayabera is actually a Panamanian shirt. The same relative berated my clothes, festive blouses and long colorful skirts. "You look like a Mexican! Can't you wear anything else?" My retort was, "I *am* a Mexican." I was also criticized for having a huge nopal growing in my front yard—"too Mexican," I suppose. How can anyone criticize a cactus? The Franklin Mountains have been called ugly by a journalist in our local newspaper. How can mountains be ugly? A local art teacher didn't know what a milagro was when I presented a cousin with one. We live so close to México and yet our Mother Culture says little to this woman. A man who lives here but is not from here is trying to sue to get the three crosses, the symbol of our town, removed from all public displays. Recently someone has informed me that when she comes into our Cultural Center, the colors hurt her. Where are the pastels, she asks? I wonder if the oscillating Our Lady of Guadalupe red and blue night-lights haven't gotten to her? They are so Mexican, so Southwestern, so New Mexican, a part of who we are as a people on the frontera. We are a people of color and music and life, and for that we should have no apologies.

So, where is the understanding of Culture? I keep asking myself.

In my travels, wherever I go I find people of all ages who are hungry for Culture. They want to know who their grandparents are, where they came from and to whom they belong. Everyone wants the energy of being and belonging.

In Oklahoma a young adopted Chicana mourns the fact that her adoptive parents won't let her date Latinos. An older woman tells me her grandfather is part Cherokee, but he never talks about it. A high school student informs me that her father is a minister but she can never write because he will never approve of what she writes. A distressed college student admits that her boyfriend doesn't like her writing and that he rewrites all her stories for her.

My advice is cold, hard and honest: Soon you will be on your own and you can date whomever you choose. Don't lose your roots. Help your grandfather to accept who he is and if he doesn't, learn about your people on your own. Don't show your father your writing. Keep your writing to yourself; it's like a fetus that needs to be nourished. I just have one thing to say to you: Please, don't let anyone take away your soul. You know who you are, so hang on and get on with it!

People want to know their roots, who they belong to and where they come from. We are all connected to someone, to something, and to know the genesis of who we are is a great blessing. It will be our rock and solace in the hard times, don't you forget it. As Cultural warriors, our greatest task is to allow others to explore their creativity without fear of censure or reproach. The greatest gift we can give each other is our lack of fear. The blessing we give each other is our tolerance, our undivided attention and our acceptance of who we are. We need to respect each other. When looked at closely, the great walls dividing us as humans are really very inconsequential. I really believe this is true.

We need to approach Culture with a tender and loving heart. It is easy to be judgmental or unkind to those who are judgmental and unkind to others. We must continue to instruct, educate, heal and empower others, who in turn will do the same.

True Culture does not divide us—instead it brings us together to explore the great mysteries that life presents us. The sometimes-difficult mysteries reveal to us our great and always present interconnection. We are all one, if only we can see this fact through the veil of perceived difference.

We have so much to be thankful for: Christmas, Hanukkah, Kwanzaa, tacos of all kinds, Pad Thai, sushi, chicken chow mein, pizza, meat loaf and mashed potatoes, mariachis, symphony orchestras, rock and roll, rap, funk, rhythm and blues, rancheras, boleros, soul music, day, night, rain, snow, blue skies, clouds, our mothers, our fathers, the many ancestors whose blood and pulse of life we carry within us.

How can I separate you from me and me from you? And if I could, would I? And why would I, knowing that completion comes from within the self because of the many selves?

Promise me, dear reader, you will begin to look at Culture in a different way. Look at and then explore your small part of this great vast world without fear and insecurity. It will reveal to you great joy, great mercy, great forgiveness and great hope.

¡Missss Rede!

"Stop that noise. Stop that and listen to me. You have no right to do that. To go off. When will you be back?

"Did I ever tell you about my honeymoon in El Paso? No, not to your Father. To Bucho Faver. Your sister's father. He was accidentally poisoned.

"Every day we went to a little restaurant. On Mesa Street. Every day we ate oysters. I didn't like them at first. But Bucho did. We were happy, Bucho and I. He was a kind man, shy. And he was very clean. He would bathe two and three times a day.

"It all started when I told my cousin Toña that I was going to marry Bucho Faver and she told someone and someone told Bucho. Delfina Rede says she's going to marry you. Shafter, Texas, was a small town and I was a teacher there. But I was more than a teacher.

"One night I was called to deliver a child. The partera was gone. As the teacher, I was expected to know, to serve, to do. I knew nothing about babies, but I boiled the water and brought that child into the world, his bright body slithering, the umbilical cord cut with a knife. He lived! He lived to grow and thank me, Miss Rede!

"Later on, there were other births, other children. This crying child was my first, as I scrambled up the hills near the silver mine, to the little house. I was a schoolteacher, not knowing about life, not knowing anything real. But how could I tell them that?

"Like the time I taught at Indio Ranch. Like the time I lived in exile, on baked earth swept clean each day. I decided to go for a horse ride. Les dije a los muchachos, get me a horse, but they were busy, so I got one myself. The horse was stubborn, mean. I struggled with him, and still he wouldn't be calmed. But eventually I got the saddle on. And that was just the beginning! That horse kicked and danced, and wouldn't be still, he bucked and ran, wild-crazy, through the mesquite and over the cerro as if fever driven, and then finally, exhausted, came back to the ranch. I was tired, but I wasn't going to let that horse take charge. Rede, I said, you can do it! And what's wrong with this horse?

"When I came back to Indio Ranch the men flocked around me, incredulous and worried. ¿Qué has hecho? They demanded. What have you done? This horse, Diablo, was unbroken, untried, Missss Rede! What have you done? Didn't you know?

"It was the same person who walked into the night to deliver Ismael Contreras Junior when no one else would. The same person who boiled water, tore strips of cloth and cut the umbilical cord with a sharp knife.

"If anyone had asked me, Delfina, can you be any happier, I would have said no. No. No. With Bucho I was happy. Now it's in heaven we'll embrace.

"Bucho got sick. He told me, 'Fina, me han matado. I'm going to die. They've killed me. The druggist gave me something. I didn't want to take it. They forced it down my throat.'

"It was me that had told him to go to the doctor. But it wasn't there that things went wrong, it was with the druggist. You know, I could have sued. But in those days, who sued? Who sued and for what? They had to hold him down it tasted so bad.

"Later he came to me. I was in the other house, our rooms, across from Mamá Gumersinda's. I was about to give birth to your sister, Faride. Bucho said to me,

'Fina, I'm sick. I'm really sick.' He knew. I was in bed and I could see him coming through the window. He was tired and stooped and sad. It was twilight and in September. Today is the anniversary of his death.

"I wasn't able to do anything. I was able to give birth to your sister. What else could I do? Bucho got sicker. Every day sicker. And he kept telling me, 'Fina, Fina, I'm dying.' Until one day he couldn't walk and he stayed in the big house. I looked through the window. The lights were on all the time. He couldn't speak anymore. He was in bed at the big house and I was across the courtyard in our little house waiting for our child to be born. Our child. September the 10th. Three days later Bucho died.

"I could have sued, but in those days, who sued?

"Everyone I've ever loved … I've cried over. Why is that? Everyone.

"That was in 1939. Today. In Shafter, Texas.

"Everyone I've ever loved I've cried for. I cried myself to sleep every night for nine years. I taught school. I traveled to México for thirteen summers. I raised Faride. But there were always those tears. Until I met your Dad. I met him and when I thought about it later, I remembered. It was the first night in all those years I hadn't cried myself to sleep.

"This is the first time I've told you about that time in Shafter. All day I've been thinking about Bucho. All day. I've got to stop. I'm tired now.

"All this loving has worn me out.

"Roll up the window.

"The man told me he'd be here soon to unlock the storage unit.

"Bucho used to bathe two or three times a day. He was very clean. He used to ask me to scrub his back. He begged me, but I refused. I was too shy.

"Now I regret not washing his back. It would have made him so happy.

"Roll up the window. It's getting cold. Where is that man? Where? Where? How long do we have to wait out here? How long?

"I was just thinking.

"Today is the anniversary of Bucho's death.

"I wish you weren't going so far.

"I know, I know. But that doesn't stop me from crying.

"When will you be back?

"Until then, your things will be safe. Don't worry. Your things will be home.

"Home.

"Come soon.

"There he is now. There he is. Isn't that someone, in the darkness, there?

"I can hear someone coming.

"Maybe that's him.

"Waiting so long, so long. I don't know. I don't mind. I don't. Mind. Not really.

"I'm used to it. "

EL CRUJIDO DE MIS HUESOS

El crujido de mis huesos
Lo ignoro por completo
Porque aun
Se soñar
Se añorar
Se amar

Lo ignoro por completo
Porque ya en lontananza percibo
La luz
La esperanza
De un mundo
Desconocido

Anhelado
Soñado

El crujido de mis huesos
Viejos, cansados,
Se ignora
Se olvida
Ya que es el pase ineludible
A esa luz imán
Que se percibe ya en la distancia
Que casi se busca
Que casi se anhela
Que ya casi se espera

I completely ignore
The creaking of my bones
Because I know
How to dream
How to mourn
How to love

I ignore them completely
Because in the distance I perceive
The light
The hope
An unknown world
Longed for
Dreamed of

The creaking of my old and tired bones
Is ignored
Is forgotten
It is the inescapable passageway
To that captivating light
Seen now in the distance
Looked for
Longed for
Almost embraced

—DELFINA REDE FAVER CHÁVEZ

Sobritas/Leftovers

TACOS 101

We're going to begin the workshop now, if everyone will come over here. Have a seat and get comfortable. We're going to talk about one of my favorite subjects: tacos. Bring your coffee or tea. Can you all hear? We'll talk a bit and then move to the kitchen area, where we'll make tortillas a mano. Following that, we'll sample a few tacos that I've made, Tacos a la Delfina—but don't eat too much because we'll be doing the grand tour for lunch: the Ranchway BBQ and Mexican Food Restaurant and, of course, dessert, paletas/popsicles, at La Michoacana. So bring your journals and take a seat. And get ready to appreciate the taco as you've never appreciated it before!

I.
La Madre del Maíz

What came first, the chicken or the egg? What comes first, the tortilla or the filling? I say the tortilla. For without a good tortilla, you have nothing. And before any taco comes the tortilla. And before the tortilla came the maíz.

The tortilla is a staple of life in the Americas, as well as in many parts of the world. It is reported that Mexicans eat over 300 million tortillas a day, and yet it has been said that the history of maíz is lost in the "night of time" (according to Professor Scherey in the book *Plants Useful to Man*).

To understand a tortilla, we need to understand maíz. Maíz (*Zea mays*) is the most domesticated and evolved plant of the vegetable kingdom, but the origins of maíz are mysterious and have been under much scrutiny. The evolutionary process of maíz is still a subject of research, because it seems to have arrived already highly evolved, with its intermediate forms unknown. In spite of much scientific inquiry, the early origins of this plant have not been found.

Maíz is the only known cereal whose wild varieties are not preserved in nature. The most popular of the theories about the origin and evolution of maíz states that the teocintle of Lake Chalco in central México (Mexican *Zea mays ssp.*) is the direct predecessor of modern maíz, but studies are still not conclusive. It has been proposed that teocintle became maíz in one single macroevolutionary step.

What can be stated is that maíz was the basic food of all American cultures long before the Europeans arrived in the New World.

Maíz is used in so many ways and forms that it has become indispensable to humankind. However, it would not grow today if it had not been planted and cultivated long ago.

Many authorities believe maíz spread from the central Andes to South and then North America and later to Central America and México. There is another theory that maíz crossed the tropical Pacific, from Burma, with seafaring navigators. It's possible we'll never know the true origins of maíz. We do know it is needed and depended upon by millions of earth's inhabitants and is a central world crop.

Geological and archaeological excavations and carbon-14 datings show ears of maize that date from 7,000 years ago in Mexican caves. In the valley of Tehuacán, to the south of México City, maíz existed 4,600 years ago and was cultivated. In pre-Columbian times maíz extended from Chile to eastern Canada. Many of the varieties existed then, and later it spread to Europe with the conquest of the Americas.

Maíz has many nutritious and medicinal properties. It is easy to digest and is very tasty. The corn tassels or "hair" have diuretic and healing qualities. The tassels have been used to assist in treating heart disease, uterine illness, prostate health and urinary disease. The tassels also serve as a food—for example, the huitlacoche, which is so valued as a tasty native food.

There are many ways to prepare maíz—it can be roasted, stewed, toasted, ground into flours and mixed into drinks. There are also more than 3,500 uses for maize products. Many soaps, cosmetics, sodas and lotions use corn as their base. Every day new discoveries are made.

We need to study the maíz plant and learn from it. It can teach us how to expand our vision of what constitutes blessing.

II.
How to Select Good Taco Meat

Look for lean, but not super-lean, ground beef: 80 percent is good. You want to have a little fat to cook the meat mixture with.

The meat should have a healthy-looking color.

Always look at your meat, unless you know that your prepackaged meat is fine. Buy from a store whose quality you know.

If you buy 4 pounds of meat, you can make a good tray or two of tacos as well as a large bowl of Granma Lupe's Pasta.

Buy meat that "blends." If the extruded meat is too rigid, pass on it. Once cooked, the extrusions should not linger. The meat should form a consistent overall mixture that then becomes a uniform mass and then separates as it is cooked.

The "binder" is crucial to any good meat taco.

III.

The Basics of a Tortilla

To have a good taco, you need to have a good tortilla.

How do you select a good tortilla? The texture should be grainy, not totally smooth, not totally bleached white, and may have some bits of corn kernel.

Some people prefer the smooth, white, thin tortillas in a package. I don't. I like my tortillas to have texture, heft. They should have a definite but not overwhelming cara.

You want a thicker corn tortilla for tacos and enchiladas.

If the tortillas have edges that look crumbly, pass them by.

Avoid any tortilla that has a pink, green or unusual hue, or mold.

Look for local tortillerías, not a tortilla maker in New Jersey, unless of course you live in New Jersey. New Jersey? Yes, someone in New Jersey is making corn tortillas right now!

Tortillas are always less expensive and fresher if you buy them at the source and in bulk.

The wraps have their place, but I am not particularly interested in eating a red #3 tortilla, either as a tostada chip or in a wrap.

Try different tortilla brands. Experiment. And see what you like. Notice what others are using. Ask around. Mexicanos are never shy when it comes to food questions. No need to be circumspect. If someone doesn't want to tell you what he or she put in their food, they won't. Don't take it personally. Cooking and eating comida Mexicana is a lifelong journey of discovery.

Disclaimer: When I speak of Mexican food, I am talking about the food I know, which is on the New Mexico/Texas/northern México border of the U.S.

IV.
Taco Essentials

A tortilla press. These can be found in Mexican grocery stores. Get a good one; no cheap imitations will do.

> *The tortilla maker consists of a pair of hardwood boards or round, iron plates joined at one end by hinges. When pressed together by a lever-like handle, the tortilla maker will flatten a ball of corn dough into a round disk. Place the dough between sheets of wax paper or plastic wrap before pressing. The paper will prevent the tortilla from sticking to the plates. Don't worry if you can't find a press. You can easily improvise one by using two cutting boards or two pie pans, some paper and enough gentle pressure to flatten corn dough into a round disc between the flat surfaces.*

> (*This good information comes from a great Mexican cookbook,* Recipe of Memory: Five Generations of Mexican Cuisine, *by Victor M. and Mary Lou Valle.*)

A comal or griddle. You can use it for roasting chile, onions, tomatoes and garlic, or for toasting spices. A large, heavy sartén, an iron pan, works well too.

If these are essential tools, then the taco ingredient essentials are: a good tortilla, a good meat or taco filling, and the right seasoning. A taco without comino/cumin is not complete. The lack of comino will make or break the best tacos.

Time and patience are irrefutably essential to cooking Mexican food. Also a good attitude. It's hard to be bitchy or angry when you are cooking comida Mexicana. A good taco session can cure the nastiest blues and remind you once again why you love life.

It helps to have a taco-cooking partner. When rolling time comes around, you'll appreciate that extra pair of hands.

V.
Things to Ponder and Remember

Cooking Mexican food takes time. Accept it. If you don't have the time to make a full-blown Mexican meal, you will have to take shortcuts: canned this, packaged that. Compromises will have to be made.

Time and love are the essence of all Mexican cooking. Think of the movie *Como Agua para Chocolate.*

Keep a bowl of water nearby to wet your hands in between making, rolling and flipping tortillas.

In case you burn yourself, keep cream or unguent nearby. More than once I've had to use a dollop of butter and spread it on a burn. Even better than butter for a burn is olive oil. Generously spread it on!

Don't take shortcuts with meat or fillings.

Check to see if the tortillas are fresh. It's best to look at them closely to see if they have mold. The mold can come in all types of colors, so watch'ale!

If you've lived in an area all your life but don't know the food where you live, shame on you! Familiarize yourself with food preparation, food buying and pronunciation of food names. It is your responsibility and gift to know about the food in the place where you live.

Tacos are sacred to me. I have been saved from depression, anxiety and more-than-serious mental and spiritual breakdown by making tacos. Cooking is therapeutic. Let go and enjoy!

Offer up the meal with gratitude and remember: tacos are one of life's greatest gifts!

Rolled tacos or folded? Your call. The answer to this question also depends on where you live and how you were brought up. If you are going to buy folded tacos, support local tortillerías.

I still can't believe that my hometown voted a well-known commercial taco chain the best tacos in town last year. Is something wrong here? What were the voting demographics? Is it of any importance it's directly next to one of our high schools?

Low-carb tacos? They are possible. Yes, they are. No oil. No triglycerides. You can learn to steam the tacos. And you must pick your fillings with care. And you can learn to avoid processed cheese and go the soy or tofu substitute cheese route. All is possible. But sometimes, just sometimes, you have to break down and "grease out." But don't feel too guilty. Pray over your tacos. I remember a curandero, a friend of our family's, Andrés Segura, who lived in México City, who used to pray over his cigarettes just before he smoked them. I saw him gingerly and prayerfully lift his cigarette, bringing it to the middle of his forehead, turning it this way and that, as he offered a prayer of thanks to the cigarette for not harming him.

Don't be afraid to try new taquerías, new restaurants and new food! Life is an exploration and a continual surprise.

Don't forget the "binder" in your tacos: peas, potatoes, corn or whatever else you choose. Be creative!

VI.
El Palote

Los palotes, the rolling pins in our family, have become legendary. They were always well taken care of and loved. I currently have about ten in my possession. They are of all sizes and widths; they can serve an adult or a child. Mother always kept them in a large drawer near the stove. Palotes have many uses other than for making tortillas and rolling out pie dough; I have opened a number of bottles by hitting them with a palote edge, and they've also served in all sorts of baking needs.

Find a palote that suits you and then use it! It helps to clean it often and, when it's not in use, to grease it down a little. With such reverence for palotes it's no wonder I still mourn the machacador, the venerable old meat masher that was stolen by one of my Father's many caregivers. If you read this and have my machacador, bring it back!

Mother made her tortillas without a recipe. She'd take handfuls of flour, add espauda/baking powder, oil and then water. I don't recall her ever having a bad batch of tortillas. Si le sobraba agua, she'd throw in more flour and if she had too much flour, she'd throw in more water. She worked quickly, without error. Sometimes she'd take off her rings to make tortillas, and I'd suggest this, except that more often that not, she'd just go into the kitchen and whip up tortillas day or night, without much fanfare.

When she finished making her tortillas, I'd clean out her rings for her. The flour mixture would have hardened a bit, and I'd take a toothpick or safety pin and clean her rings. My Mother's and Father's silver wedding rings came from Taxco, one of her favorite Mexican towns.

I still have my parents' wedding rings, both of them cleaned out. I was always doing strange and unusual errands and jobs for Mother, and she was grateful. I found nothing odd in it. I cleaned out her rings, painted her fingernails and curled her hair when she had a particular hairdo for about a year or so with short side bangs. I shined her shoes, was her errand girl and girdle finder. I pulled her toes for her as well. Mother was arthritic and always needed work on her feet and legs. I also rubbed her legs and feet when she had calambres, cramps. Mother had worn a girdle for many years, and no doubt this constricture contributed to her vein problems and exacerbated her condition. She was in constant pain from her legs, and although my sisters and I wore girdles for a short while, we never had the purple red veins Mother developed over the years. We are leg-compromised, however, and this comes from standing so much. I always have to stand to work.

Most Mexican food is best made standing. Don't ask me why. Unless you are rolling tacos with a partner or making tamales en masse, our cooking requires standing and a lot of to and fro activity.

VII.

A Good Cheese Grater

How do you like your cheese grated? What's your preference? Do you like your cheese thick or thin? What kind of cheese do you like? I prefer a cheese that melts. Like the extruded meat, there is an extruded cheese that doesn't melt. Cheese isn't the same as it used to be. What happened to cheese? Find a good cheese: Monterey Jack or Longhorn or a combination is good. Find a good cheese grater that grates cheese not too thin, not too fat, and remember: the cheese always goes on last. The French handheld cheese graters are great for individual tacos, but the small cheese output isn't good for a large tray of tacos. Blanket the tacos in the tray with average-sized cheese.

Allergic to cheese? Use soy or lactose-free cheese or crumbled tofu or better yet, forget the cheese and add other things on top: tomatoes, lettuce, aguacate. Cheese is not totally essential to Mexican cooking, though it really is a big part of it. You have to accept that or learn to make healthy substitutions, which can be done in a creative manner.

This touches on the lard question, which is very subjective. I don't use lard in tacos, nor do I shy away from them if they are offered by well-intentioned people who use lard. I don't offend those who use lard, since I grew up with it.

I understand many people use lard and it doesn't frighten me. I use lard for my biscochos, the sugary holiday cookies. I know lard and don't it eat often, but let's face it, it can be a valuable asset in Mexican cooking. Tamales are always better with lard and so are biscochos. I leave the ultimate decision to you.

VIII.
El Sartén

No one pays enough attention to the condition of the frying pan these days. Mother's was old, seasoned—in other words, it was a wonder. She cared for it but not too much. It's said you shouldn't wash your seasoned frying pan with soap, but she did. She did dry it off, but that was about it. I don't remember her oiling the pan to keep it in good shape. Her motto was: Care for things, but not too much. I guess that's how I see things as well. Remember the past, but don't get lost back there. Celebrate the blessings of the past in the present, but remember to live today. Today is built on the past and tomorrow is evolving from both the past and the present. The future? ¿Quién sabe? Hopefully, there will always be tacos.

IX.
The Taco Brigade

Before we climb in our cars and vans to go eat, let's remember the many blessings in this world, including one of the most sacred: tacos. Thank you all for joining us for Tacos 101. I really have enjoyed this workshop. May you continue to learn about that great and powerful plant, maíz, and come to really appreciate her companion, the mighty taco.

Does everyone have his or her agenda? So who is going with whom? All I know is that I don't want to drive. The Ranchway? *You've never been to the Ranchway?* Caray, how long have you lived here? Take a left at the Dairy Queen on Valley Drive. Go north about six blocks. It's on the right-hand side. The grey building with the turquoise trim. They're waiting for us. We're in for an adventure!

X.

PRAYER TO LA MADRE DEL MAÍZ

Madre del Maíz
Mother of the Maíz
Sacred Mother
Mother of the Earth, her children

We thank you for the grace of your gifts to us:
Maíz: the five holy sisters—
Red, blue, white, speckled and yellow—
They are the races of the earth and they are good.

Madrecita, you who have created blessing
You who are blessing
Feed us, nourish us and prepare us
For the final blessing of earth

You who dreamed us, it is to you
Maíz Mother we are grateful

Madre del Maíz
Holy Mother who dreams worlds
Tender Mother who holds life in her hands
Kind Mother who feeds her children
Far-seeing Mother who wants to see her children
Nourished, sustained, uplifted and healed

We bless you
We bless you
We bless you

Te bendicimos
Te bendicimos
Te bendicimos

Glossary

a mano—by hand

abrazo—hug

acequia—irrigation ditch

agotada—exhausted

agregarle un poco—add a little

aguacate—avocado

ahí voy—I'm coming now

albóndigas—meatballs

algo para la familia—something for the family

aperitivo—before-meal food or drink

arroz—rice

asadero—soft cow's milk cheese, good for melting

asco—disgust, nausea

así es—so it is

atole—thick corn beverage

ayudante—helper

azul—blue

bandejas—pans

barbacoa—barbecued meat

Basilica de Nuestra Señora de Guadalupe—
    Basilica of Our Lady of Guadalupe

bendición—blessing

bien—well

biscochos—sugary cookies often served at
    Christmas and other festive times

biznaga—barrel cactus; candy made from its pulp

blanco—white

bolillos—crusty white bread rolls

bordón—walking stick

botana—appetizer or snack

buche—gullet, cow gullet

¡Buen provecho!—roughly translates as "Enjoy
    your food! Bon appétit!"

bueno—good

cabra—goat

caca—poop

cada cosa en este mundo tiene su trabajito—
    everything in this world has its work/its
    reason for being

cajeta—a confection of caramelized milk

calabacita—zucchini squash, a delicious squash
    dish

calambres—cramps

calaveras—skulls

calcetín—sock

calientita—nice and warm

"Canción Mixteca"— a well-known Mexican song

capirotada—bread pudding

cara—literally face, the side of the tortilla that hits
    the comal/griddle first

caray—gosh!

cerro, cerrito—hill, little hill

cesos—brains

Changó—one of the Orisha, an aspect of God in
    the Santería religion

chapulines—grasshoppers

chicharrón—fried pork skin

chichis—breasts

chile con queso—chile with cheese

chiles rellenos—stuffed green chiles

chisme—gossip

chones—underpants

chorizo—spicy sausage

chucherías—junky trifles

chupacabra—goat sucker (mythological monster)

colmo—the utmost/the be-all and end-all

colonia—neighborhood

comadre—the godmother of your child, or a close
    female friend

comal—griddle

comida—food

comida corriente—daily special

comida de casa—home cooking

comida mexicana—Mexican food

comino—cumin

compadres—close friends

compañeros—companions

consejo—helpful hint, tip

corazón—heart

creo en mi familia—I believe in my family

cruda—hangover

cuales están listas—which [ones] are ready

Cuauhtémoc—Montezuma's nephew, the last
    Aztec ruler, murdered by Cortez

cuchispete—shameless hussy

cucuy—boogeyman

cuento—story, tale

cumbia—Mexican dance rhythm

curandera/curandero—folk healer, curer

de vez en cuando—every so often

delantal—apron

delicioso—delicious

Depresión—the Depression

descanso—roadside memorial

desenpanse—after-meal digestive

desgraciadamente—disgracefully

después—after

Día de Los Muertos—Day of the Dead, All Souls
    Day, November 2

Diez y Seis de Septiembre—September 16, a
    patriotic holiday in México commemorating
    the revolution against Spain

dulce de camote—sweet potato candy

echar un grito—utter a joyous cry

el otro lado—the other side (of the U.S. border)

empanadas—pastry turnovers

ensalada—salad

entre mundos—between worlds

entremeses—hors d'oeuvres

espauda—baking powder

esperanza—hope, expectation

espina—spine, thorn

Estados Unidos—United States

federales—Mexican federal policemen

fideos—noodles with tomato sauce

fiel—loyal, faithful

flauta—a long fried rolled taco

frijoles—beans

frijoles a la olla—beans boiled in a pot

frijoles refritos—refried beans

frontera—border

fulano de tal—so and so, what's his name

gracias a mi familia—thanks to my family

grito—cry

güango—loose

güisar—to flash fry

güiso—something that has been flash fried

hecho en México—made in Mexico

hechos a mano—made by hand

hermana—sister

hoy en día—nowadays

huitlacoche—corn fungus used as a food

intercambios—exchanges

jamás—never

juicio—judgment, good sense

La Llorona—a weeping woman in the folk legend,
    who drowned her children

labio—lip

lagarto—alligator

las de deveras—the real ones

lengua—tongue

les agradezco todo—I appreciate everything

les dije a los muchachos—I told the boys

limón—the essential lime that wakes up all
    Mexican food and drink

limpia—clean, or a cleansing ritual

limpiador—dishcloth

lo Mexicano—things Mexican

luminarias—folded paper bags holding votive
    candles

m'ija, m'ijita—a term of endearment for girl or woman given by someone older

m'ijo, m'ijito—a term of endearment for a boy or man given by someone older

machacador—food masher

Madrecita—dearest mother

madrina—godmother

maíz—corn

mañana—tomorrow

mano—hand

manteca—lard, shortening, fat

manteca vieja—old cooking oil, drippings

mantequilla—butter

mariachi—a singing, strolling Mexican band

más—more

masa—dough used for tortillas

me han matado—they have killed me

mejor—better

mejor unos tacos—some tacos would be better

mera mera—one and only

mercado—market

Migra—slang term for people who work for the immigration service

mil gracias—a thousand thanks

milagro—miracle, or a small amulet

mios—mine

Misa del Gallo—Midnight Mass

mitote—gossip

mocosa—squirt, pipsqueak, kid

mojados—a derogatory term for people who cross the river, wetbacks

mole—a savory Mexican sauce, often made from chocolate and red chile

molote—a bun hairstyle

morcilla—blood sausage

mordida—bribe

muchacha—girl

mugre—filth

mujeres indígenas—indigenous Indian (Native American) women

muy de moda—very fashionable

nalgas—buttocks

nativos—natives

negro—black

ni modo—it doesn't matter, "whatever"

Niño Fidencio—the child Fidencio, a Mexican folk saint

no es posible—it's not possible

¿no quiere unos tacos?—don't you want some tacos?

no tengo tiempo—I don't have time

nomás—not only, no more than

nomás para probar—just to try

nopal, nopales—prickly pear cactus

nopalitos—dish prepared from cactus pads

nuevo—new

nunca—never

ojo de Dios—a yarn decoration named for the eye of God

olla—pot

¡órale!—right on! listen up!

pa' la comida de mi gente—for the food of my people

pa' mi viejito—for my old man

padrino—godfather

paleta—popsicle

palote—rolling pin

pan—bread

pan dulce—sweet bread

partera—midwife

¿pero cómo?—but how?

pésame—condolences

piloncillo—firm brown sugar in a pressed cube

piña—pineapple

piñata—papier-mâché or clay figure filled with toys, candy, etc., used at parties

pitayas—Indian figs, fruit of the nopal or cactus

plato especial—special dish, "the special"

plato fuerte—main dish

pleito—argument, fight

policía—police

polvo—dust

polvo legítimo contra la maldad—a folk remedy
to counteract evil

por el amor de Dios—for the love of God

por favor—please

postre—dessert

puesto—vending cart or booth

pura/puro—pure

puras indias—pure Indians (Native Americans)

que Dios lo cuide—may God protect him

que Dios nos cuide—may God watch over us

¿qué has hecho?—what have you done?

qué lástima—what a pity/shame

qué rico es la comida de mi gente—how delicious
my people's food is

que viva el taco—long live the taco!

querida suegra—beloved mother-in-law

quesadilla—a folded tortilla with melted cheese
inside

queso Menonita—Mennonite cheese

¿quién sabe?—who knows?

rabia—anger

raíces—roots

raja—strip of green chile

raza—race or culture

rebozo—shawl

res—beef

Sagrado Corazón—Sacred Heart

sal—salt

Santería—syncretistic religion of Caribbean
origin, originated in western Africa

sartén—a heavy iron frying pan

si le sobraba agua—if you have leftover water

siempre—always

sin nada—with nothing

sin vergüenza—shameless

sobrino—nephew

sobritas—leftovers

sopa caldosa—hot soup

sopa seca—"dry" soup, rice or pasta

sopaipilla—fried bread puff

susurro—whisper

tacos de deveras—real honest-to-goodness tacos

tamalada—tamale-making gathering with family
or friends

taquería—taco restaurant

taquero—taco maker

te agradezco todo y tanto—I appreciate
everything and all things

te bendicimos—we bless you

te saludo—I salute you

teocintle—possible ancestor of maíz

tía—aunt

tierra quemada—burned or baked earth

tinita—container, little tin

tío—uncle

toalla—towel

toalla sanitaria—sanitary napkin

toda la familia—the whole family

todavía me duele—it still hurts, emotionally

toque—touch

Toritos—a cocktail made with fruit juices and
alcohol

tornillo—screw

tortilla de harina—wheat flour tortilla

tortilla de maíz—corn tortilla

tortillería—tortilla shop

travieso—mischievous

tripas—tripe

tu hermana en ese camino de cultura y
reconocimiento—your sister in that road of
culture and remembrance

vato loco—crazy dude

vecinas/vecinos—neighbors

vecindades—neighborhoods
velas—candles
¡ven!—come!
vengan a comer las tortillas—come and eat the
    tortillas
vestida de luto—dressed in mourning (black)
viejita—little old lady

viejito—little old man
vino tinto—red wine
watch'ale—Spanglish slang term for "watch out"
y—and
ya están listas—they're ready!
¡zas!—bang!

List of Recipes

¡Mil Gracias!

I am very grateful to my publishers, Susan and Ross Humphreys, for believing in me so completely without even seeing so much as a chapter to flap in the wind. It has been a great joy to work with these wonderful friends and publishers and their amazing press. Thank you for becoming compadres!

I want to thank Susan Humphreys for agreeing to be my editor. Thank you, Susie, for your insights and many kindnesses and for listening so deeply. It is a great gift you have given me with your attention and thoughtful insights. Te agradezco todo y tanto, comadre.

Thanks to my vecinos, Eliza and Roberto Frietze, who have taught me what Culture really is and how very gracious and kind the human heart can be.

Friends come and go, and the older you get, few really remain that are fiel but can still kick your nalgas when you need them kicked. I thank those compañeros who have walked with me when the fields of friendship have become dry: Sandra Cisneros, Benjamin Alire Sáenz, Richard Yáñez, Genevieve Chávez, John Randall and Robert Con Davis Undiano. Un abrazo to dear friend César González for his insights into the translation of the poem "El Crujido de mis Huesos." As he said to me so profoundly, "Lovely poem … great sense of approaching the horizon's blade."

Special thanks to my sister, Margo Chávez-Charles, who helped me to remember some savory details and helped me to translate the untranslatable.

Thank you to the Lannan Foundation for their support over the years and encouraging so many world border writers to write their truth.

There aren't enough words to thank Elsa and Jesus "Chuy" Rodriguez from the Ranchway BBQ and Mexican Food Restaurant, my dear friends and supporters in so many adventures. They have fed and nourished me for many years and I am so grateful. Thanks as well a toda la familia "Ranchway": Elsa, Chuy, Chico and Michael Rodríguez; Rafael "Veco" Monge; Julia S. Domínguez; Elvira Soto; and Marina Moreno for the best food in the world and the extra gifts of potato salad and guacamole. ¡Les agradezco todo!

New friends are among the graces of life, and I want to thank Estela Reyes for her consejos as well as Gina Nuñez for her light-filled meditation that showed me how to tame the wild beasts. Mil gracias to Sylvia Bejarano and her invaluable manteca vieja insights and to those helpful friends who have contributed to these taco tales: Kathy Gallegos Austin, Jorge Robles, Laura Robles, Ellen McCracken, Melinda Palacios, Melissa Flores and Jerry Wright.

¡Te saludo, Ricardo! My thanks to Ricardo Aguilar Melantzón, fellow writer and compadre de corazón, who gave so much to the borderland he loved so much. Your memory is sacred. We shared meals at El Ranchway more than a few times. I wish you eternities full of tacos and love.

Thanks to Marthe Zolinsky, my mother-in-law, a sweet and gentle woman who taught my husband and his brother, George, how to be good men, great cooks. May you rest peacefully, querida suegra!

Thank you to Mayor Michael Cadena for his support and friendship these past years as well as the Town of Mesilla, New Mexico, for becoming my favorite place in the world.

Special thanks to my husband, Daniel Zolinsky, for helping me roll tacos for over twenty-one years! I have appreciated his incredible meals over time and his support in many ways visible and invisible. Also, the man has taught me how to cook and that deserves a grito!

Blessings and eternal love to my parents, Delfina Rede Faver Chávez and E. E. "Chano" Chávez. I bless and thank you both for giving me life and tacos.

To all you taco-istas out there, I hope you have enjoyed this memoir in food. ¡Buen provecho!

Tu hermana en ese camino de cultura y reconocimiento,

—DENISE CHÁVEZ
Las Cruces and Mesilla, New Mexico
La Frontera entre Mundos

¡Qué Viva El Taco!

Acknowledgments

Some of the work in this book previously appeared as follows:

"A Family of Feet." *Frank: An International Journal of Contemporary Art and Writing*, 1998.

"I Am Your Mary Magdalene." *Chicano Creativity and Criticism: Charting New Frontiers in American Literature*. Houston, TX: Arte Público Press, 1988.

"La Macha Grande." *Sí Magazine: Latinos in the Arts, Fashion, Entertainment and Politics*, Summer 1996.

"Mejor Unos Tacos." *Lannan Foundation Program*, 2003.

"Mercado Day." *Mexico Poetry Renaissance*. Santa Fe, NM: Red Crane Books, 1994.

"Missss Rede." *The Journal of Ethnic Studies*, 1987.

"Missss Rede." *Women Writers of the Southwest, Walking the Twilight II*. Flagstaff, AZ: Northland Publishing, 1996.

"A Taco Testimony." *The Ink Arts Newspaper*. Las Cruces, NM, March 2001.

"Tilt-a-Whirl." *Resiembra: An Anthology of Chicano Literature*. Española, NM: Conjunto Cultural Norteño, 1982.

List of Photographs